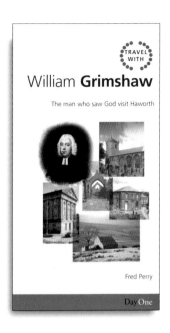

TRAVEL
WITH

William **Grimshaw**

The man who saw God visit Haworth

Fred Perry

Day One

D1387356

Series Editor: Brian H Edwards

Day One

TRAVEL
WITH

William **Grimshaw**

33

❸ Taught by a pedlar

Although Grimshaw exercised a firm discipline over the inhabitants of Haworth, they warmed to his sincerity. A spiritual revival began that transformed the village, but his friendships and actions prompted the nickname 'Mad Grimshaw'

Grimshaw's predecessor at Haworth had been Isaac Smith. Smith had paid for the rebuilding of the church barn and had contributed half the money towards installing the church clock. He had also dedicated 'Soudens' as the parsonage, splashing holy water on it, shouting loud acclamations, praying and making signs of the cross. But the vestments he chose and his eagerness to collect his financial dues really alienated the congregation.

Although the Haworth trustees had been happy to enlist the help of Benjamin Kennet, the vicar of Bradford, in their disputes with Smith, they did not want him interfering with the appointment of a new minister. Kennet thought he had the authority to appoint and took the Haworth trustees to the Archbishop's court in York. The trustees won the case and so, after almost eleven years at Todmorden, Grimshaw became the perpetual curate of Haworth on 16 May 1742. For most practical purposes, a perpetual curate has a similar security to that of a vicar and performs largely the same role, unlike temporary curacies where a

Above: The bleak hills around Haworth

Facing page: St Michael and All Angels, Haworth—the 15th century tower is the oldest part—the rest of the church was demolished in 1879 and rebuilt

93

❼ Roughed up at Roughlee

Grimshaw suffered emotional and physical blows but they failed to deter him from his calling. He won a war of words with George White after being attacked by his 'army'

Grimshaw travelled with Benjamin Ingham and his assistant William Batty to take a service in a house in Colne on 9 July 1747. They noticed a threatening crowd gathering round their leader and vicar, George White, at the entrance to a tavern and when the three entered she knew they expected trouble—and it soon came. They had just begun to sing the opening hymn

when White and the mob forced their way in and went for Batty. The three escaped into another room and overheard the vicar and constable threaten the householder with the stocks. As they attempted to carry him out, the man asked what authority they had to do this. The constable admitted that he had no warrant and promptly released him. The people who had gathered for the

Facing page: The Market Cross (replica), Colne

Above: St Bartholomew's where George White preached his sermon against the Methodists in July 1748

CONTENTS

● Meet William Grimshaw 5

© Day One Publications 2004 First printed 2004

All Scripture quotations are taken from the Authorized Version

A Catalogue record is held at The British Library   ISBN 1 903087 68 6

Published by Day One Publications Ryelands Road, Leominster, HR6 8NZ

☎ 01568 613 740 FAX 01568 611 473 email—sales@dayone.co.uk www.dayone.co.uk   All rights reserved

Design and Art Direction: Steve Devane Printed by CPD

Dedication:To my wife Jean for her patience in listening to Grimshaw for forty years or more

Meet William Grimshaw

On the wild borders of Yorkshire and Lancashire lived a man who began his career as a minister in the Church of England by swearing only in 'suitable company', and when drunk, sleeping it off before going home. His visits to parishioners were spent chiefly hunting, fishing and playing cards. William Grimshaw's life was changed in a remarkable way, but soon he suffered a heart-rending bereavement that threatened to break him completely. Gradually overcoming this tragedy, he began to throw himself energetically into his work. When he arrived in his new parish, few had any interest in true Christianity, but within a few years up to a thousand would walk for miles over bleak moorland to gather for a service of communion. On what he called 'an idle week', he rarely preached more than fourteen times, but on 'a busy week' rarely less than twenty-eight!

A strong, enthusiastic man with a keen sense of humour, Grimshaw spoke in the dialect of his congregation and possessed an iron will and forceful personality—often he literally drove his parishioners out of the alehouse and into the church with a horsewhip! Yet his deep sincerity and humility meant that as a caring pastor he was greatly loved by his people. His large heart and peaceable spirit influenced the formation of five non conformist churches in the district, and he set up the first Methodist Circuit.

John Wesley, the Methodist evangelist, hoped that Grimshaw would be his successor and commented that, 'A few such as him would make a nation tremble.' Later, the fame of Haworth—which in the eighteenth century was solely due to Grimshaw's work—drew Patrick Brontë and his family to the village.

Facing page: William Grimshaw, an engraving from a portrait by a Haworth artist

1 A Parson out of his depth

Although born into a family of legendary dragon-slayers, his upbringing and early ministry gave no indication that God would use William Grimshaw in an exceptional way. But he was destined to do immense damage to the cause of 'that old serpent, the devil'

The quiet Lancashire village of Brindle had seen turbulent times. It is claimed that in AD 937 the golden haired Athelstan won a great victory there over the Dane Anluf and his army who invaded via the Ribble estuary. In those days, the river was the main highway from Viking York to the Irish Sea, and in a fierce battle five kings and seven earls were killed. Athelstan was the first king to be crowned on the King's Stone at Kingston upon Thames in AD 925. The largest Viking treasure outside Russia, the Cuerdale Hoard containing 80lb (36 kg) of bullion and over 7,000 silver coins, was discovered on the riverbank nine hundred years later. The Vikings may have buried it as they beat a hasty retreat from the estuary. The greater part of the hoard is in the British Museum although parts of it are scattered throughout 170 places in Britain.

A divided community
In 1580 the Lord of the Manor of Brindle, who was a Roman Catholic, was imprisoned in the Tower of London for supporting Mary Queen of Scots against Elizabeth I. In order to raise

Above: detail of the South window at St James' Church, Brindle in Lancashire

Facing page: St James' Church, Brindle where William Grimshaw was christened in 1708

Below: The tombstone of Grimshaw's father at Brindle

Above: A Viking Attacked—a mural on the front wall of the Cavendish Arms (see page 18)

money to secure his release, he sold the manor to the Protestant Cavendish family. Brindle continued to have a large proportion of Roman Catholics and was Royalist during the civil wars. In 1651, Cromwell's cavalry arrived and Colonel Lilburne made St James' Church his headquarters, tethering the horses in the meadows behind the church. One night twelve local men attempted to steal the horses but the guards killed all except one, who hid in a tree.

Grimshaw was born in Brindle on 3 September 1708, to parents who were nominally Christian. His father was churchwarden at St James' church under an elderly vicar who apparently made no great impact on the parish during his long tenure—his death was recorded in the parish register as 'exit Mr Piggot, Rector'. At the time that Grimshaw was born, the civil wars had ended almost sixty years previously and subsequent legislation had resulted in the majority of Puritan ministers being forced out of their livings.

William Grimshaw was born at a time of unrest when, following the upheavals of war, some of the

The Great Ejection when the church lost its soul

After the restoration of the monarchy under Charles II in 1660, Catholic bishops were restored to their dioceses and were determined on revenge against the Reformers who had exposed the shortcomings of their church. Although Clarendon, the Lord Chancellor, had hoped that his 'Code' would encourage the church to broaden its outlook so that there would be freedom of conscience to all, the crown and traditional clergy would have none of it. An Act of Uniformity in 1662 required ministers to renounce the reformation that had taken place, to wear vestments and to assent to every part of *The Book of Common Prayer.* It is estimated that 2,000 Puritan and Presbyterian ministers and schoolteachers were evicted from English parishes and a third of all ministers in Scotland. The loss of these godly men who had replaced pomp and ritual with the centrality of the Scriptures and the necessity for godly living was incalculable. The accession of William of Orange to the throne in 1688/9 changed English history in a decidedly Protestant direction.

Above: Burying the Cuerdale Hoard—a window in the Cavendish Arms

old certainties had gone and had not been satisfactorily replaced. People still knew which families had been Royalist or Parliamentary supporters, and it was only twenty years since William of Orange had taken the throne of England. This had provoked further division as supporters of James II hoped for a return to the line of the Stuart kings. Brindle was almost equally divided between Roman Catholics and Protestants, and the first Jacobite uprising (the Stuart supporters) had ended in defeat at nearby Preston in November 1715 when Grimshaw was just seven years old. He therefore grew up in an area of divided loyalties and in a land where the future political outcome was uncertain.

In the nearby Hoghton Tower, there is a room where candidates for the Roman Catholic priesthood were hidden before journeying on to the seminary at Douai. It is possible that George White, who subsequently became Grimshaw's bitter enemy, was once concealed there.

An inadequate preparation

Grimshaw's education began in the schoolroom that used to be in the churchyard. First he joined the set that was given only a basic education, but he was later promoted to the group at the other end of the room where he learned Latin and Greek. Grimshaw then went, via Blackburn Grammar School and Heskin Free School, to Christ's College Cambridge where he was admitted as a 'sizar', or poor student. Apparently supported during the first year by friends of the family, he was then awarded a scholarship.

In Grimshaw's day Christ's College was in decline and had only about sixty students. He was one of the three youngest admitted. Most of the limited annual intake of between six and ten were from the north of England. The college mainly

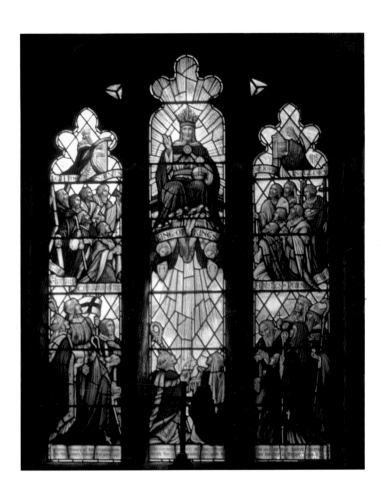

Above: East window St James'

Below: St James' and Cavendish Arms, Brindle

trained schoolmasters, but Grimshaw had made up his mind to enter the ministry. Such a life was the best that someone from his background could aspire to, although he felt no call to such a position or to a life of piety, which is understandable given the lack of role models in the church of his day.

Grimshaw was a good student for the first two years, but supervision and teaching were very lax and he drifted into the careless life typical of his fellow

Above: Hoghton Tower where candidates for the Roman Catholic priesthood were hidden during Grimshaw's youth

students. Those who were appointed to instruct the students spent much of their time on their own interests and so the education offered was left to tutors who were originally meant to be the students' guardians. Grimshaw found discipline to be erratic and without logical structure: there were fines for shaving on a Sunday and public flogging for swimming in the river Cam, but no penalty for 'what not' with the town girls. However, he did achieve his Bachelor of Arts and came down from Cambridge with habits of 'drinking and swearing and what not', although careful not to offend those who had helped him financially. He swore only 'in suitable company'—which was the people to whom he was naturally drawn.

Above: Christ's College, Cambridge, where Grimshaw studied

Through the help of Dr Samuel Dunster, Grimshaw was offered a curacy in Littleborough. The high church disciplinarian Dunster also gave him some books and seems to have had a lasting influence on him. With the offer of a church, William was now able to apply for ordination and was duly ordained a deacon by the Bishop of Chester on 4 April 1731 in the private chapel in Queen Square, Westminster. He appears to have been the only candidate on that occasion and the solemnity of the service made a deep impression. William later said that he had been: 'much affected with a sense of the importance of the ministerial office, and the diligence that ought to be used in the discharge of it.'

Littleborough was a small hamlet on a road junction. The church where he ministered has been pulled down and nothing of note is known about his ministry there. He was no more than five months at Littleborough before he changed places with an old friend who was having difficulties in combining work in the Todmorden parish with his duties at Rochdale Grammar School. Littleborough was six miles nearer to Rochdale. St Mary's Church at Todmorden, which became Grimshaw's charge, has since been enlarged and has undergone a number of alterations, some quite recent. There was a parsonage overlooking the cemetery but Grimshaw did not use it until he was married. Initially he chose to lodge with the Lacy family at Stones, a mile or so up the hill from St Mary's.

In Grimshaw's time, Todmorden was a hamlet set in the Calder valley where the road from Rochdale came down the hill and crossed the river before climbing again to the Bradford and Keighley area. Here there was little more than the church, Todmorden Hall, a few cottages

Above: *The courtyard at Hoghton Tower*

Above: View of Todmorden from the railway station

and the White Hart Inn. Although there was a 'horse track' in the valley bottom connecting Todmorden to Hebden Bridge, at that time there were generally no real roads in the damp valley bottoms and there was danger from the wild boar. The highways were the old stone-flagged routes on the hilltops with minor roads following the contours of the hills. The chief homes were therefore in the hills. This meant that Grimshaw would have a good deal of travelling to visit his parishioners and some of them would have a long journey to church. The area in general was thought to be a wild and savage one which strangers entered at their peril. Ralph Thoresby wrote at the time: 'The inhabitants of the district between Halifax and Todmorden are as wild, uncouth, and rugged as their native hills; and indeed it is positively dangerous for a person to pass that way.'

This kind of lawlessness attracted people such as the 'coiners' who chose to live in isolated houses in nearby Cragg Vale. They clipped gold from guinea coins, melted that gold to make other 'guineas', and were so ruthless in protecting their interests that they murdered an excise man in Halifax in 1769. The local inhabitants feared them and their power was such that their leader was known as 'King' David Hartley.

The main highway in the area was the Long Causeway, an ancient roadway linking Burnley and Halifax via Luddenden. The track occasionally dips to cross tributary valleys but never down into the steep Calder valley itself. It was the main transport artery in this region for many centuries until roads and the canal were built in the valley after Grimshaw's time. In his day it was a busy route, but with traffic in both directions, passing was difficult owing to the narrowness of the track. Here there would be packhorse trains with padded wooden saddles carrying lime, coal and iron, and especially bales of cloth *en route* to what were known as piece halls where the cloth would be sold, such as that at Heptonstall. Each locality along the way had a responsibility to keep the Causeway in good order. If one did not do so, neighbouring localities would take them to a local six-monthly court where they would be required to put their part of the Causeway in order before the next court sitting. Today the route is mostly for cars but the original track remains in some places.

An inadequate parson

The deep impression of Grimshaw's ordination soon faded and he became a 'hunting, shooting and fishing parson'— happier in the company of his drinking companions than in his role as curate. A year into his incumbency at Todmorden, and at the age of 24, William was ordained as priest at Chester Cathedral; he could now perform weddings and administer the Lord's Supper. This event appears to have passed without repeating the impact of the first ordination. It would not be long before his inadequacies were revealed.

Early one morning William was called out to Lodge Hall in Walsden, the home of James and Susan Scholefield. The couple had been married for a number of years before their eagerly awaited

Above: The White Hart at Todmorden. The market and court of petty sessions were held here in Grimshaw's day. The present building dates from the early 20th century. A fair was held here in 1750 and the constable was allowed eighteenpence for cleaning his truncheon and a shilling for 'walking the fair'

Above: Part of The Long Causeway near Bank Top Farm, little changed from Grimshaw's day apart from the modern wind farm

first child was born. Tragically, during the night, Susan Scholefield had laid over her daughter, accidentally suffocating her. When the parson arrived, Susan was walking around the hall in a daze, cradling the baby in her arms and making baby talk to her as if she were still alive. James, the father, was distraught, and explained that Susan had been walking like this since she found the little one dead. Grimshaw was helpless. Finally, he told them to: 'Put away those gloomy thoughts, go into merry company, divert yourselves, and all will be well at last.'

It is easy to imagine the bewilderment of the parents and the embarrassment of Grimshaw over his inability to be of any help. Nevertheless, the Scholefields called him out once again and this time he confessed that he was in no better spiritual state than they were: 'But to despair of the mercy of God would be the worst of all.' Subsequently the Scholefields found peace with God, being converted during a service of Holy Communion at the church at Cross Stone, a few miles away from Todmorden. They started a meeting in their home area of Walsden, and James eventually became a Methodist preacher. They had another daughter and in faith called her Mary, the same name as the child they had lost.

Grimshaw's advice to this couple reveals something of his mind-set at this time. Rather than facing up to the big issues of life, he was distracting himself with the various diversions of the world. But at a deeper level, he was aware of his own inadequacy although without any notion as to how he could do anything about it. Reflecting on this incident in later years, Grimshaw admitted

that at that time he had been a blind leader of the blind.

Disguised as the devil

Another incident concerned a young man who was unwilling to support his pregnant girl friend. This was a serious issue with potentially grave consequences for the girl in question. Sometimes the parish would agree to support the mother and child but, if the pressure brought to bear on the father-to-be failed, or as often happened, he ran away from the area, the girl could be driven out of the district so that her support would be borne by some other parish. For example in nearby Heptonstall, the father of an illegitimate child had absconded and, recognising that the mother and child would become a charge on the township, the Overseers of the Poor had decided to act as 'father of the bride'. They organised a posse and searched the local villages and towns until

Above: The bar at the Cavendish Arms. Parish meetings were held here in Grimshaw's day

they found the man, arrested him, and brought him back to Heptonstall where he was by some means or other persuaded to marry the mother. The account book reads:

> To arresting the bridegroom
> 10 shillings;
> Payment to the bridegroom as
> inducement to marry 10
> shillings;
> The Minister 5 shillings;
> Wedding Reception 14
> shillings and 10pence;
> Miscellaneous 5 shillings and
> 10pence;
> Total Two Pounds Five
> Shillings and Eightpence.

All this was much cheaper than the alternative of the parish caring for the unfortunate girl.

Therefore the problem Grimshaw was facing was typical at the time. Many young men managed to evade the overseers of the poor by running away and joining the army. Faced with the same dilemma and unable to persuade the errant youth by other means, Grimshaw dressed up as the devil and waylaid him on his way home one night. Only when the terrified young man agreed to marry the girl if the devil would let him go did Grimshaw release his grip. Mrs Lacy, William's landlady, subsequently discovered the mask and cows horns and Grimshaw confessed to his subterfuge. Although it had the desired effect, Grimshaw was rightly ashamed of what he had done.

For the first few years of his ministry, Grimshaw was completely at home in the social

Above: The gateway of Hoghton Tower

set of those who went hunting, shooting and fishing, and played cards in the local hostelry. This was a continuation of his behaviour at the end of his Cambridge days. He was popular among this kind of company, offered no threat to their way of life, and by his conduct actually endorsed it. He thought himself conscientious in his discharge of his duties as a parson—after all, he never entered the pulpit in a drunken state. He really had no idea regarding anything deeper than the formalities of religion. When crises arose in the lives of his parishioners, he was found sadly lacking. William would also be found lacking when the great crisis of his own life occurred.

Above: Interior of Cavendish Arms

TRAVEL INFORMATION

Brindle

OS Grid Reference SD 595245

St James' church

Dating from the 15th century, this church has five fonts, some beautiful windows, and boasts the two oldest ringable bells in Lancashire, cast about the year 1490. The ringers were sometimes paid in ale when the landlord of the *Cavendish Arms* was also churchwarden. The empty stone coffin, said to have contained the remains of one of the kings killed at Brunanburgh can be found outside the church at the north east corner wall.

The Cavendish Arms

This building owned by the church was sold in 1921. The vicars may have lived there until Henry Piggot built a rectory in 1690. Many church meetings have been held in the inn and in the 18th century, drink was considered to be a legitimate expense. There are many small rooms in the house, most of them with stained glass windows depicting Athelstan's victory. Meals are served from 1200 to 1415 and evenings 1730 to 2200 except Mondays. ☎ 01254 852912

Brindle by car from Blackburn

Take the A674 then the right fork on to the A6061 then the A675. Turn left off A675 at the Brindle sign. Approximate distance 5 mi (8 km) From the M65, exit Junction 3 then A675 towards Preston, turning left at the Brindle sign. Approximate distance 4 mi (6 km).

Hoghton Tower

OS Grid reference SD 622264

A fortified hilltop manor house, the ancestral home of the de Hoghton family since the 11th century. William Shakespeare started his

working life here. There is a Tudor well house (horse-drawn pump/oaken windlass); underground passages associated with the Lancashire Witches; wine-cellar and dungeons, and a special dolls' houses exhibition.

Open to the public July to September, Monday to Thursday 1100 to 1600; Sunday 1300 to 1600. Car Parking. 'Phone to confirm ☎ 01254 852986

By car from Brindle

Go back to the A675, turn left and in about 0.5 mi you will see the entrance to the Tower on your right.

HOGHTON

3

A 675

TO
M6 (J 29)

B 5256

M 65

BRINDLE

1

2

KEY TO PLACES

1   ST JAMES' CHURCH
2   CAVENDISH ARMS
3   HOGHTON TOWER

Above: The gateway of
Hoghton Tower

❷ Over the edge

Grimshaw's greatest happiness was in his marriage to Sarah, but her early death threw him into near insanity—until he read a book that changed his life

Sarah Sutcliffe was two years younger than Grimshaw and had been married twice, losing both husbands in the first year of marriage. She was a spirited young woman and started flirting with Grimshaw. They probably first met when they were both out riding. Certainly she used to ride to his lodgings regularly and shout, 'Mr Grimshaw I am come to bid a penny at you', which in those days was almost an invitation to marriage. When he heard her voice, they would ride out over the hills together. One thing they did have in common was a sense of humour; throughout his life William loved practical jokes. He was a strong and energetic young man, but for all her outward bravado Sarah was a sick woman and perhaps felt protected in his company. There is no doubt that they fell deeply in love.

The success in finding Sarah and being accepted by her and her wealthy family took his mind away from the failures in his role as parson. Years later he was to write in his unpublished *Experiences Gather'd by Conversation with my own and the Souls of Others*, that the marriage of an immature Christian couple could inhibit

Above: The seventeenth century St Mary's at Todmorden, from the west

Facing page: The South aspect of St Mary's

their growth as Christians and was therefore best delayed until they were well established in the faith. However, they married and settled down in the damp parsonage in the churchyard. The wedding probably took place on the 9 June 1735 as that is the endorsement on the marriage bond, but there is no record of it in the area. A son, John, was born a year later and daughter Jane in the following year. Both were named after Sarah's parents, although by that time her mother had died and her father had remarried. Sarah suffered from what was called 'consumption'— the disease generally known as 'tuberculosis' although there is a possibility that in that area it was a euphemism for alcoholism. Whatever the cause, she was a sickly woman and perhaps had a number of periods away from Todmorden, recuperating in the luxury of her parental home. Jane was probably born there because she was christened at the family church at Luddenden. It is also likely that John, being the first child, was also born there although he was christened at Todmorden. These recurring bouts of illness and absences would put an extra strain on Grimshaw and further distance him from his work in the parish,

Grimshaw's instructions concerning his burial

The first paragraph shows his deep devotion for Sarah and the last expresses a stronger hope than he really had at the time of writing.

'The Form of My Burial.

Whenever Almighty God is pleased to receive my soul unto Himself, I require my executors to bury my body in the same grave with my deceased wife, Sarah, in the chancel of Luddenden; or if that be impracticable, then either in the church or church-yard of Luddenden aforesaid, as near her as convenience will permit.

To attend my funeral I desire that 20 persons be invited (of my next relations and intimatest acquaintance) and entertained in the following manner:—Let 5 quarts of claret (which will be every one a gill) be put into a punch bowl, and drunk in wine-glasses round till done. Let every one have a penny roll of bread to eat therewith; let every one come, and let all sit down together to the same as an emblem of Christian love.

This at home.

Let every one have a quart of ale, a 2 penny spiced cake, and afterwards, immediately before rising up, a glass of claret and a paper of bisket (4 papers to the pound); distribute the biskets first, then the wine. This at the drinking-house …

(there follows an expenditure account for the funeral, totalling £5).

In this form I hope my executors will bury me, as I hope to rise again to a blessed resurrection, through the merits of my dear Redeemer, Jesus Christ.

Nov 26 1739

W. Grimshaw'

Above: The balcony in St.Mary's where Grimshaw's family sat

especially as on these occasions he would take time off to visit the family.

Sarah was very good for Grimshaw emotionally but was probably of little help spiritually. His *Experiences* may reflect on this time when he wrote: 'Where husband and wife observe prayer in their family, to frustrate that exercise and the blessings attending it, Satan will prejudice the wife against her husband for praying, so the husband will be prevailed upon to leave off. This is a grievous and dangerous device of the adversary.' The *Experiences* were, of course, written with the benefit of hindsight and from a more mature spirituality, so these observations may not have been in his mind at the time referred to.

Nevertheless, there were spiritual stirrings. William became concerned for his soul, afraid that he was destined for hell, and began praying four times a day—a habit he maintained until his death. Imposing strict self-discipline, he earnestly tried to live a righteous life. He fasted regularly and kept what amounted to a spiritual account book where he would put sins in the debit column and attempt to at least balance them by the good works he could enter in the credit column. It was also at this time that he made a solemn covenant with God. He repeated this practice at certain stages in his life and quarterly towards its end. People, including Sarah, called him a saint, but he did not understand the true Christian message. One person on hearing him preach betrayed his position by concluding: 'He took us to hell and left us there.'

Death of Sarah

Suddenly disaster struck. On the 1 November 1739 Sarah, the love of his life died, a little into the

Above: Interior, St Mary's

concluded the Bible was a book of fables. God was cruel and implacable; Jesus had been a mere man. Even with his heart aching for Sarah, he lusted after every woman he saw. Suicidal with internal turmoil, he still kept up the appearance of the dutiful clergyman. The will he wrote in the same month of Sarah's death gives no indication of his inner struggles. The conflict of rebelling against God and yet still deep down knowing he was doing wrong, produced painful physical symptoms as well as the fear that he was going insane. The pressure would have led to a serious mental breakdown but for the intervention of the grace of God.

It may seem morbid for a young man to be dwelling on his death, but in his day, long life was not as assured as it is today, the average life expectancy was 35–40 years. Even as he matured as a Christian, Grimshaw found it beneficial to think about death. He later wrote, 'Think and meditate much on the last things—Death, Judgement, Hell, Heaven. To think of death is death to some men … meditation on death will put sin to death. There is a way to keep a man out of hell; but no way to get a man out of hell.'

During his near insanity after Sarah's death, William controlled himself before his parishioners on all but one occasion. That day he was in the pulpit and blurted out: 'My friends, we are all in a damnable state, and I scarcely know how we are to get out of it!' This could have been the result of reading *Precious Remedies Against Satan's Devices* in which

fifth year of their marriage. Grimshaw was heartbroken and his reformation fell to pieces. The relationship with Sarah had been deep and strong, they had two lively young children, and much to look forward to as a family. There were the Lockwoods to help look after the children, but nobody to take the place of Sarah. His religion though sincere, had been on the surface: concerned with doing things he believed would gain the Lord's favour. This tragedy seemed to him as though his good works were all to no avail—God had disowned him.

Grimshaw retaliated. He was tempted to blaspheme, to curse God and to belittle his wonders of creation. He had been misled and

Above: Scaitcliffe Hall—where Grimshaw felt the heat

Thomas Brooks set out 36 strategies of Satan and 200 ways to overcome them. Unfortunately, although Brooks said that believers needed to repent of being discouraged by their sins, the effect of his book on Grimshaw was to drive him further into despair.

Light in the darkness

Early in 1741 Grimshaw visited a friend at Scaitcliffe Hall, Todmorden. As he was talking to this man he took hold of a book, opened it, and suddenly felt a flash of heat. He was some distance from a shelf on which there were pewter objects and was sure that the sun could not have reflected that distance from them, but to test it he turned around the other way—and felt the flash again. This book was by another Puritan author, John Owen, *The Doctrine of Justification by Faith*. Grimshaw was given permission to take the book home—and it changed his life.

Grimshaw described the impact of the book: 'I was now willing to renounce myself, every degree of fancied merit and ability, and to embrace Christ only for my all in all. O what light and comfort did I now enjoy in my own soul, and what a taste of the pardoning love of God.' The Bible became a new book to him. He said it was: 'As though God had drawn up my Bible into heaven and sent me down another one.' The symptoms that had accompanied his depression disappeared and he was full of health and joy.

Then the elation wore off and William lost the initial joy and wondered if he really had been born again. What he called his 'constitutional weakness'—a yearning for an intimate relationship with a woman—built up a pressure he had to relieve. He descended into another depression until he realised that losing the first flush of faith was a common Christian experience. He compared it with Jesus being led into the desert to be tempted after the exaltation accompanying his baptism.

Just under two years after Sarah's death, Grimshaw married Elizabeth Cockcroft. She, like Sarah, came from a wealthy land-owning family. Grimshaw's brother John, who was married to Elizabeth's sister, made the introductions and William had spent some time at the large house called 'Mayroyd' set in its own grounds 1 mile (1.6 kilometres)

from Hebden Bridge. Little is known about the relationship between Grimshaw and Elizabeth, partly because it lasted only five years and was overshadowed by spectacular events in that time, but also because it seems to have lacked the intensity that characterised his first marriage. Perhaps it was a marriage on the rebound.

Throughout the period between the marriages and for long after, Sarah's family, the Lockwoods, were a source of real support. Often the children were lodged with them at Ewood, high above Mytholmroyd on the northern side of the Calder valley,

The Message that changed Grimshaw's life

Dr Owen, who was at one time a chaplain to Oliver Cromwell, describes the content of his book in its full title: *The Doctrine of Justification by Faith through the Imputation of the Righteousness of Christ; explained, confirmed, and vindicated.* This is a large volume and, like other books by Owen, not an easy read. In it, he explains that there is nothing we can do to justify ourselves in the eyes of God. Only if we have a right understanding of the absolute majesty and holiness of God can we see ourselves as we really are. When we have some understanding of who he is, we realise how impossibly far away from him we are because of our sin. Owen writes, 'The best of men when they have had near and efficacious representations of the greatness, holiness, and glory of God have been cast into the deepest self-abasement, and most serious renunciation of all trust or confidence in themselves.' Our only hope is for a mediator between God and ourselves, and God has provided the Lord Jesus Christ to be just that. Our sins have been charged to him, he has borne our punishment, and when we put our trust in his sacrifice for us on the cross, we are judged to have his righteousness. Only that righteousness can satisfy the absolute holiness of God. We therefore need to relinquish all hope of being justified with God by our efforts and to put all our trust in Jesus Christ who has reconciled us to God. Owen backs his argument with many quotations from Scripture.

Above: *These windows at Scaitcliffe Hall were probably there in Grimshaw's time*

and Grimshaw would make frequent visits to be with John Lockwood and his family. John in particular also took a keen interest in Grimshaw's ministry and was later to open his home to preachers such as John and Charles Wesley and George Whitefield. He also designated Grimshaw's children, John and Jane, as his heirs.

To the wild people and bleak moors of Haworth

Shortly after his second marriage, Grimshaw received an invitation to become vicar of the church at Haworth. He probably thought it would be advisable to move away from Todmorden with all its memories of Sarah and to make a

fresh start with Elizabeth. Six months later they arrived in Haworth and there he began his remarkable ministry.

Haworth, set on a steep hillside, was even less civilised than Todmorden. The population of less than three thousand were a wild, unruly, and fiercely independent people. Most worked in their own small businesses in the worsted trade. They would scour, comb, and spin the wool, weave and then wash the cloth and hang it to dry outside the house on 'tenterhooks' (a 'tenter' was the wooden frame on which newly woven cloth was stretched, and 'tenterhooks were used to fasten the cloth to the frame—from the Latin *tentus*

Above: Todmorden's municipal splendour

'stretched'; the word now has the metaphorical meaning of being held in suspense). Living accommodation was downstairs and the work was done in the upper room. There was no sanitation, and human excrement flowed down the sides of the steep Main Street. It is little wonder therefore that Haworth was a notoriously unhealthy place, with many children dying in their first few years and the average life expectancy was as low as twenty-five. The churchyard bears testimony to these grim facts.

TRAVEL INFORMATION

Todmorden

OS Grid reference SD 940241

Situated on the western edge of Yorkshire, on the river Calder and the Rochdale canal, this busy market town used to be a major cotton processor, the machinery being driven from streams pouring down the three steep glaciated valleys that meet in the town. A major walking route, the Pennine Way, goes through the town. There is an open market Wednesday, Friday, Saturday, and Sunday with a fleamarket on Thursdays. The indoor market is open Monday to Saturday, but Tuesday is a half-day.

Todmorden Town Hall

This is Todmorden's most impressive building and was built during Victoria's reign. Before the county boundaries were redrawn during the late 19th century the building was half in Lancashire and half in Yorkshire. The pediment supported by Greek columns has two women as the central figures, the left hand representing Lancashire and the other Yorkshire.

St Mary's Church

The oldest church in Todmorden, dating from the 17th century is situated in the centre of Todmorden on the junction of the main roads. Although screens have been removed and the church modernised, there are still some old features. Tradition says there is a passage from Todmorden Hall to the church. One of the incumbents before Grimshaw was Henry Krabtree who began his tenure in 1666. He was the first man to undertake scientific observations of

Above: *The seventeenth century Todmorden Hall: Once a home, then a Post Office (1924), now The Old Hall Restaurant*

Pictured: *The Rochdale Canal runs between Manchester and Sowerby Bridge in West Yorkshire,. At Sowerby Bridge it connects with the Calder and Hebble Navigation. The canal was re-opened to navigation along its entire length in July 2002*

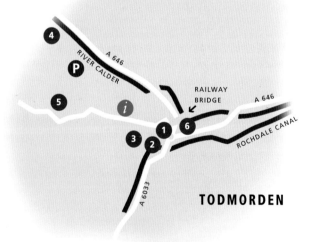

KEY TO PLACES

1 ST MARY'S CHURCH

2 TODMORDEN OLD HALL

3 RAILWAY STATION

4 SCAITCLIFFE HALL HOTEL

5 TODMORDEN HALL FARM

6 TOWN HALL

Todmorden Hall

the transit of Venus. He was also an astrologer who made predictions in the church register: 'James, son of James Taylor of Todmorden. He was born … near sun setting and also full moon which is a sure sign of a short life.' Some said he was a wizard. There is a story that he saw a mouse in church, took it as a sign of disaster, stopped the service and rushed home to find his house being burgled.

Todmorden Hall

This is a fine example of 17th century domestic architecture. It has linenfold panelling and an original front door with a bolt for every day of the year. Having been a private residence it then became a post office, and is now *The Old Hall Restaurant*.

Scaitcliffe Hall

Dating from the middle of the 14th century, the present Hall was reconstructed in 1821 although it retains some older features such as stained-glass windows. It is on the A646 Burnley road out of Todmorden about 1.5 mi (2 km) on the left. It is now called Scaitcliffe Hall Hotel. ☎ 01706 818888

Todmorden by road

Todmorden is situated approximately 10 mi (16 km) from Halifax or Burnley on the A646.

Todmorden by rail

There is a rail service between Manchester Victoria and Halifax, Bradford and Leeds that calls at Todmorden.

Pictured: *Scaitcliffe Hall*

❸ Taught by a pedlar

Although Grimshaw exercised a firm discipline over the inhabitants of Haworth, they warmed to his sincerity. A spiritual revival began that transformed the village, but his friendships and actions prompted the nickname 'Mad Grimshaw'

Grimshaw's predecessor at Haworth had been Isaac Smith, who had paid for the rebuilding of the church barn, and had contributed half the money towards installing the church clock. He had also dedicated 'Sowdens' as the parsonage, splashing holy water on it, shouting loud acclamations, praying and making signs of the cross. But the vestments he chose and his eagerness to collect his financial dues really alienated the congregation.

Although the Haworth trustees had been happy to enlist the help of Benjamin Kennet, the vicar of Bradford, in their disputes with Smith, they did not want him interfering with the appointment of a new minister. Kennet thought he had the authority to appoint and took the Haworth trustees to the Archbishop's court in York. The trustees won the case and so, after almost eleven years at Todmorden, Grimshaw became the perpetual curate of Haworth on 16 May 1742. For most practical purposes, a perpetual curate has a similar security to that of a vicar and performs largely the same role, unlike temporary curacies where a

Above: The bleak hills around Haworth

Facing page: St Michael and All Angels, Haworth—the 15th century tower is the oldest part—the rest of the church was demolished in 1897 and rebuilt

person acts under the supervision of a rector or vicar.

However, the trouble with Kennet did not end there. He had a right to collect money from the parish at Easter and other times, a practice that seemed unfair to the Haworth congregation. One of the churchwardens was excommunicated twice for not allowing Kennet to see the register so that he could work out what was owed to him. When he learnt of the increased congregations under Grimshaw, he felt that much more was owed him; and he probably wanted his revenge for the embarrassing result at the Archbishop's court! Grimshaw was technically subordinate to Kennet, his vicar, although in practice this does not seem to have had much significance because, as was the case with Isaac Smith,

Kennet preferred to involve the Archbishop in disciplinary matters.

Ignorant of the growing storm, the Grimshaw family moved into 'Sowdens'. It was a low building set into the hillside above the church and the plague-ridden village. The air was certainly better there and the house had its own plentiful spring which was an advantage over most of the village houses where people had to walk some distance to one of the water pumps. Furthermore, although its significance was not realised at the time, the village supply of water seeped through the graveyard before it reached the pumps! So, there was a cycle of death, out of the graveyard and into it again. Later, Patrick Brontë, whose new parsonage also had its own fresh stream, campaigned long and

Above: St Michael and All Angels, Haworth

Above: William Grimshaw's parsonage—now a private house

hard before a decent water supply was provided.

Although Grimshaw was a strict disciplinarian, the Haworth people gradually warmed to this strong, blunt young man, perhaps because like them he was not afraid to speak his mind. Also he did not put on airs and graces and he spoke in the local dialect. Another point in his favour was that unlike Smith and Kennet he did not insist on the poor people paying his dues. However, when he arrived there were only twelve communicants, and it was some time before he would see more than: 'a few souls … affected under the Word, brought to see their lost estate by nature and to experience peace through the blood of Jesus.'

Others were preaching the gospel in the North of England at that time. Benjamin Ingham, who had been a member of the Wesley's Holy Club at Oxford, returned to his home town of Ossett, a few miles south of Leeds, and began preaching in his mother's home, then in a number of other houses. He was later ordained and sailed to Georgia to evangelise the American Indians with the Wesleys. On his return, Ingham grouped people together for fellowship and mutual support and established over fifty of these societies in his travels through Yorkshire and Lancashire. John Nelson, a stonemason converted under John Wesley, was another evangelist. Grimshaw, however, was the only preacher of the gospel with a parish ministry.

Revival at Haworth

Grimshaw entered his new duties wholeheartedly. The people of Haworth were soon aware that this was a man with a pastor's heart who was not out to feather his own nest at their expense. Gradually they were moved by his preaching and lifestyle and were interested to find out more. In less than six months after he arrived at Haworth, there was an outpouring of the Holy Spirit. Grimshaw explained it well: 'In 1742 … our dear Lord was pleased to visit my parish.' It was an act of sovereign grace, so much so that the church that only had twelve communicants in June 1742 was within a year crowded with over 900 people and many more standing outside. Hundreds from other parishes trudged miles across the bleak moors to satisfy their curiosity or renew the blessing they had already received. Grimshaw cast himself in the role of spectator when he wrote, 'Here, as in other places, it was amazing to hear and see what weeping, roaring, and agonies many people were seized with at the apprehension of their sinful state, and the wrath of God.' There seems to be a link here with the work of Ingham and Nelson. God was at work and he chose men like Grimshaw, who were in one way or another earnestly seeking him.

But Grimshaw was more than a spectator; God was doing a work in his own life. He had a new understanding of the Bible, rose every morning with the doxology, read the appointed Scriptures for the day, and then led a prayer meeting for his household. This meeting was to continue for the rest of his life at 5 am in the

Benjamin Ingham

Benjamin Ingham troubled Grimshaw in his early days at Todmorden by implying that William was a Pharisee building on the sand of his own works. Grimshaw became very nervous of Ingham's presence and avoided him whenever possible; if his coat caught on a briar he would be afraid that it was this man again, for he always laid a gentle hand on his shoulder. Ingham had returned to England with the intention of finding more recruits for the Georgia mission, but nearing his hometown he received a special anointing of the Holy Spirit for evangelising that area. He then exercised a powerful ministry in the churches where he was initially very welcome and crowds came to hear him. Later he was brought before an ecclesiastical court in Wakefield and forbidden to preach in the churches of Yorkshire. Ingham helped John Nelson in the early days of his ministry but then they had a disagreement. He also separated from the Wesleys and joined the Moravians. Although Grimshaw feared his rebuke at first, he was able to welcome Benjamin's presence later and acknowledged that he and John Nelson had been the first ones moved by the Holy Spirit in what was to become a great awakening in the area.

Left: Main Street Haworth—possibly the inspiration for Ann Brontë's hymn: 'Believe not those who say the upward path is smooth'

summer and an hour later in the winter. Four times a day he went aside from the busyness of his life to be alone with his Lord and he finished the day at 11pm after family prayers. He would close morning household prayers with his benediction: 'May God bless you, in your souls and in your bodies, and in all you put your hands to this day! Whether you live or whether you die, may the Lord grant that you may live to him, for him, and with him forever!' His preaching was earnest and compelling and, speaking in the common dialect, had a directness that many other ministers lacked.

But this earnestness was not just in the pulpit. So keen was Grimshaw that the whole of Haworth should be in church to hear the word that, during the singing of the psalm he would go out and drive reluctant parishioners into church with a horsewhip! Sometimes he would send his churchwardens on the mission, and it is said that on one occasion when they had not returned he went out to find them; he reappeared in church holding both wardens by the ear and announced to the congregation: 'Look what I found in the alehouse!' Someone travelling through Haworth on a Sunday morning was startled to see people jumping out of the windows of the *Black Bull*. He enquired if there was a fire and in reply they shouted that the parson was after them. This practice of 'whipping in' was not as unusual as might be thought. At St Bartholomew's church in Colne, where George White, Grimshaw's implacable opponent was vicar, as soon as the second lesson started the churchwardens rose as a body and staff in hand went out into the town. The constable preceded them and the sexton followed behind wielding a whip to drive all the idlers they could find back into the church. The sexton was also required to whip dogs out of church.

The church is too small

These bizarre methods must not hide the fact that God continued to bless Grimshaw and his ministry, and within the year plans were in hand to enlarge the church without raising any money from the Haworth parishioners. To do this, Grimshaw had to carry his Trustees with him, and jointly they had to ask permission from the church authorities. The reason for the proposed extension was that so many were coming from other parishes to find the spiritual food that was not available to them at home. Grimshaw realised that accommodating people from other parishes would not be seen as an acceptable objective, so the

Above: The King's Arms—the meeting place of the turnpike committee and a place to hide from the parson

Above: The Black Bull—no refuge from the whip here!

reason he gave was, 'For the open and orderly Attendance of Publick Service of Almighty God, wherein we are greatly interrupted and disturbed by too crowding a Congregation.' Permission was granted but unfortunately the finance was slow in coming and the additions could not be completed until 1755. Meanwhile Grimshaw removed a window on the north side of the church near his three-decker pulpit and erected scaffolding so that he could step on to the outside platform at times during the sermon to enable those in the churchyard to hear him better. But with all the tremendous awe that had descended on the place, and the overflowing blessing resulting in many conversions, Grimshaw was still not confident of his own salvation.

Grimshaw imposed a very strict observance of the Lord's day. In addition to compelling people to come to church, he insisted that they behave properly once there. If he was saying prayers and he noticed someone not paying attention he would stop, address the offender, and would not proceed until he was sure all in the crowded church were settled in the proper attitude. The prayers were to him a vital part of the service and had to be offered unhurriedly and with all reverence. On one occasion, he saw people reaching for their hats during the benediction: 'Let your hats alone,' he shouted, 'they'll stay if you let them!'

Besides preaching to his large congregations, he began his 'monthly visitations' in 1743. He described them to John Wesley in a letter of 1747: 'I visit my parish in twelve several places monthly, convening six, eight or ten families in each place, allowing any people of the neighbouring parishes that please to attend the

Scotch Will

George Whitefield said of him: 'At Haworth, I met William Darney who has since been imprisoned for preaching. Though he seems unqualified, yet I met with many that date their awakening from first hearing him.'

Darney wrote: 'I have known by happy experience, that I have been in the greatest extremity of suffering for my dear Lord and Master's sake; when I did not expect to escape with my life; God in his rich mercy and wisdom; always made me a way of escape. I have found the most of God's presence when the sons of wickedness have been permitted to abuse my body and tear my clothes in pieces. I have at times tasted the martyrs' cup, praised be my God who counted unworthy me worthy of this honour for his name and Gospel's sake. There was one time in particular when the persecutors had taken and tumbled me over head and ears into a nasty hole, full of mire, with my enemies dancing and pushing one another on top of me. Indeed I was infinitely more happy than all my enemies could have been. I found such a manifestation of God's love as made me that I found not pain but I experimentally felt something of heaven in my soul.'

Scotch Will's Cottage

Exhortation. I am now entering into the fifth year of it; and wonderfully, dear Sir, has the Lord blessed it.'

There were also smaller meetings in his parish. If a person seemed to be inattentive in church, he might point to him and shout, 'We shall meet in this man's house next Tuesday.' To those who were reluctant to attend church he would announce that he was coming to hold a service in their house. 'I know I am not welcome,' he would concede, 'but I will speak to everyone under my care concerning his soul, if you will not hear me at church you shall hear me at home.' They knew he was serious when he phrased his determination in the Yorkshire dialect: 'if yer determined to perish, yer'll perish wi' t'sound o' t'gospel in yer lugs!'

So impressive was his bearing that although the people loved him, they also feared him. On one Sunday, a man travelling on horseback through the village went to the blacksmith as his horse had lost a shoe. The blacksmith would not do the job without Grimshaw's permission so he took the rider to Grimshaw and when the man said that he was hurrying to fetch a midwife, Grimshaw gave permission for the horse to be shod. The market day in Bradford was traditionally on a Sunday and the parson had a hard job changing people's habits but he succeeded—as he did with the youths who had always played football on a Sunday afternoon. Grimshaw would play with them during the week but would not allow them to do so on a Sunday.

Top: *Cottages in Haworth where Grimshaw visited his parishoners*

Left: *Town End Farm (around 1600) the hub of a haulage business in Grimshaw's day*

He was strict but, using the authority that was given to parsons in his day, he was strict only for the things that he felt mattered most and in this way impressed their importance on his flock. There was nevertheless tenderness in his imploring people to turn to Christ, and though the people of Haworth might think him rather odd, he did win the affection of the majority.

Scotch Will

One well-known lay preacher in the area was William Darney, a huge, red-haired Scottish shoemaker and peddler who had been converted in the awakening in Scotland in 1739 and had subsequently received 'an uncertain call to preach' which was later strengthened. He is described as carrying a pack and selling handkerchiefs, stockings and suchlike. He gave reading lessons in lieu of paying for his lodgings, and preached the gospel at the various places where he put up for the night. Will had an unjustifiably high opinion of his skills as a poet and made up verses for his hosts in the hope that they would buy them. But in spite of his faults as a poet, he was a strong and courageous evangelist. When he came to preach in a house near the church gates, Grimshaw determined to stop him as, at that time, he believed that preaching was not an occupation for those who had not been ordained. He muscled into the house with the intention of disrupting the meeting and disciplining those present, but became so impressed by what was being taught that he stayed on. When the rest of the people had left, Grimshaw arranged to meet Darney early in the morning at the local quarry to discuss matters of doctrine. He duly arrived there the next morning, fearful of being seen meeting with Darney, and possibly because Elizabeth, who had no sympathy with what he was doing, would have further scorned his meeting with a peddler.

Grimshaw, though preaching the message of the Bible to good effect, felt himself a hypocrite: 'How can I preach justification and the new birth when I am a stranger to these things and under the wrath of God myself?' Darney replied, 'You must preach them till you experience them; and then preach them because you know and enjoy them.' There is no doubt that these clandestine meetings were a help to Grimshaw. Later when Darney preached in the open air, Grimshaw was bold enough to go with him and give out the hymns. The word went round the village that 'Mad Grimshaw has become Scotch Will's clerk.'

Above: The quarry where Grimshaw secretly met with Scotch Will

TRAVEL INFORMATION

Bradford

Bradford used to be a centre of the wool trade. The Wool Exchange still stands on Market Street but it now houses shops. There are two railway stations, Forster Square (for Keighley) and Bradford Interchange (for Halifax, Todmorden) about half a mile apart. The latter houses the bus station.

Cathedral Church of St Peter

Near the Forster Square station. In Grimshaw's day this was a parish church known as 'the church in the woods'. Buildings have since replaced the woods. Although now extended, this is a modest Cathedral compared with most.

National Museum of Photography, Film and Television

Near the Bradford Interchange. A large exhibition of the development of the camera, one on the development of television with some 'hands on' experience for children, and various other permanent and touring exhibitions. There is an Imax cinema with usually seven shows featuring different films during the day and two in the evening, and Pictureville and Cubby Broccoli cinemas which between them show between 5 and 7 different films a day. There is a charge for the cinemas but entry to the museum is free, although sometimes there is a charge for a special touring exhibition. The museum is open 1000–1800 from Tuesday to Sunday each week but only opens on a Monday during main school and bank holidays. There is a

Top: *Church Bank, Bradford*   **Above:** *Bradford Cathedral*

Above: *The National Museum of Photography, Film and Television*

shop, snack-bar and restaurant and the Pictureville Café Bar for those attending the evening films open 1700–2100. Booking and enquiries ☎ 01274 202030 www.nmpft.org.uk

Haworth

OS grid reference SE 036372

Haworth by road

Take the A6033 from Keighley and after approximately 3 mi (6 km) follow the minor road to Haworth.

Haworth by bus

Services 663, 664, 665, 698 and 720 leave from Keighley bus station. Keighley and District buses ☎ 01535 603284

Service 698 also leaves from Bradford interchange. For Metro Bus routes and rail travel in West Yorkshire ☎ 0113 245 7676

Haworth by rail

Trains from Bradford (Forster Square) and Leeds go to Keighley. Change here for Haworth on the preserved Keighley and Worth Valley Railway.

Angels' Church

The people of Haworth have worshipped here for about 700 years although the present building is not much more than 100 years old. Relics of Grimshaw's ministry are a pair of pewter flagons (not on display), the Communion Table and the Candelabra in the Brontë chapel, and the stone font in the churchyard. Patrick Brontë's ministry was the longest in the history of the church. He commenced in 1820 and ministered for 41 years. There are many mementoes of the Brontë family in the church and the family vault contains the bodies of all of them with the exception of Anne who was buried at Scarborough.

Pronunciation?

Haworth is pronounced as 'Howuth'–'How' as in *cow*.

Above: 'Sowdens' from the farm

'Sowdens'

Grimshaw's parsonage is best approached in dry weather via the church footpath leading up the hill and past a car park. Approaching by road, take the Colne road out of Haworth and turn left along Cemetery Road (signed Penistone Hill) then immediately left again into Dimples Lane (signed Oxenhope), 'Sowdens' is on the left shortly afterwards, about 10 minutes walk from the church. Please note that 'Sowdens' is now a private house.

Brontë Parsonage Museum

This is the Georgian home of the Rev. Patrick Brontë and his family. It is furnished as it was in the sisters' day and has several of their personal items. Open April to September 10.00–17.00; October to March 11.00–16.30. Closed 24–27 December and 7 January–1 Feb. ☎ 01535 642323.

Apart from the church and parsonage, the other places associated with the Brontës lie outside the

Above: Home of the Brontës

Left: *Haworth churchyard: trees were planted by Brontë's successor to relieve the bleakness*

village. There is a well-signposted walk across the bleak moors to the Brontë falls (2½ mi) and then a further 1½ mi to the ruined Top Withens which some associate with Wuthering Heights. The path is uneven in parts and can be muddy, walking shoes are advised.
www.bronte.org.uk

The Brontës

Patrick Brontë was born one of ten children to a poor Irish farmer on St Patrick's Day 17 March 1777. At 16 he opened a school and at age 25 entered St John's College, Cambridge where he obtained his Bachelor of Arts four years later. He married Maria Branwell the daughter of a prominent Cornish Methodist in 1812. After a short curacy in Essex he was vicar at Hartshead and Thornton before moving to Haworth on 25 February 1820. Although it was over 50 years since Grimshaw's death, the place was still famous for his ministry and that was the attraction for Brontë moving there. By that time Patrick had published four small books, mostly of verse. Maria, his wife, died of cancer 15 September 1821. Four years later the Brontës' two eldest children Maria (11) and Elizabeth (10)

The Brontë sisters

Patrick Brontë

died after contracting fever at boarding school in Cowan Bridge (Lowood in *Jane Eyre*). Charlotte, Emily and Anne became famous writers, at first under assumed male names. Their works are still enjoyed today: Charlotte is best known for *Villette, Shirley,* and *Jane Eyre;* Emily for *Wuthering Heights;* Anne for *The Tenant of Wildfell Hall.* Their young brother, Branwell was a gifted artist and writer but wasted his talents on opium and alcohol. The *Black Bull* was where he spent much of his time in Haworth. Patrick became blind in 1846 and died 7 June 1861 aged 84 having outlived his wife and all their children, none of whom lived longer than Charlotte who died at the age of 39. There is now a huge international interest in the Brontës and there are usually visiting groups from overseas, especially Japan, which has an annual Brontë day on 6 June!

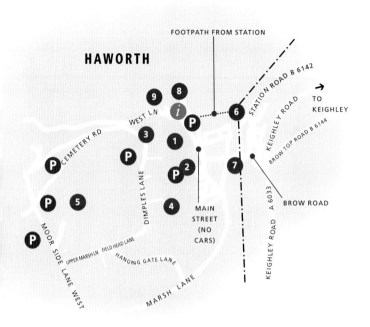

HAWORTH

FOOTPATH FROM STATION

WEST LN

STATION ROAD B 6142

TO KEIGHLEY

KEIGHLEY ROAD

BROW TOP ROAD B 6144

CEMETERY RD

DIMPLES LANE

MAIN STREET (NO CARS)

BROW ROAD

KEIGHLEY ROAD A 6033

MOOR SIDE LANE WEST

UPPER MARSH LN   FIELD HEAD LANE

HANGING GATE LANE

MARSH LANE

KEY TO PLACES

1   ST MICHAEL AND ALL ANGELS
2   BLACK BULL (WITH CAR PARKING)
3   BRONTE PARSONAGE MUSEUM
4   SOWDENS FARM
5   PENISTONE HILL
6   RAILWAY STATION
7   BRIDGEHOUSE
8   WEST LANE BAPTIST CHURCH
9   WEST LANE METHODIST CHURCH

THE BRONTE FAMILY VAULT IS SITUATED BELOW THIS PILLAR, NEAR TO THE PLACE WHERE THE BRONTËS PEW STOOD IN THE OLD CHURCH. THE FOLLOWING MEMBERS OF THE FAMILY WERE BURIED HERE MARIA AND PATRICK. MARIA, ELIZABETH, BRANWELL, EMILY JANE, CHARLOTTE.

Above: Brontë Vault in Haworth Church

❹ The Vision

The work spread beyond Haworth and Grimshaw attracted opposition from fellow clerics. He established firm links with ordained and lay evangelists and a remarkable experience transformed his life

Scotch Will, like Ingham, had set up little societies of believers who met together to pray, have fellowship and encourage each other. The societies would be put in the charge of one of the members who was a man of prayer. Will would visit these 'Darney Societies' in the course of his travels and give them a word of encouragement. Grimshaw also began to visit three of them regularly: Heptonstall every sixth Sunday; Widdop every fourth Tuesday, and Luddenden every fifth Friday. He also visited each of the four hamlets in his own parish three times a month. His concern for his flock at Haworth was broadening and he was keen to take every opportunity that offered itself to him, even if it meant holding meetings in private homes, which was an unusual departure for an Anglican minister. House meetings however, were starting up in many places within the region because of the work of the Holy Spirit. Such meetings were all the more remarkable given that people were at work for up to fourteen hours a day.

John Wilkinson, a poor shoemaker, had been to hear John Wesley's convert, John Nelson,

Above: Fire in the Black Bull

Facing page: Main Street, Haworth—much as it would have been in Grimshaw's time except for the 'New Age' shops which he would not have allowed!

and was converted. Although he had only minimal education and little Scripture knowledge, Wilkinson set up a meeting in his house at Keighley. Thomas Colbeck, a young man who at the age of twenty was running his own business in Keighley, had seen the change in the young man's life and was amazed to hear that he was preaching, so he hid in the next room to where Wilkinson was holding forth. When he heard the message, Colbeck was convicted of his sin and yielded his life to the Saviour. He then devoted his life to spreading the gospel in the region around Haworth, funding himself through the proceeds of his shop. One of the first things he did was to organise a meeting in Haworth for Nelson's converts. Colbeck, a thin and zealous young man became a co-worker with Grimshaw who affectionately called him 'spindleshanks.'

Grimshaw the disciplinarian

One reason why Grimshaw regularly visited the hamlets was to contact the people who made the lack of decent clothes an excuse for not going to church. It also gave the old and infirm an opportunity to worship and hear the word as he visited their homes. Although preaching to hundreds, Grimshaw did not neglect small groups or even individuals. He had a responsibility for their salvation and took it seriously, even to the point of invoking the discipline of excommunication if he thought it would help.

Although he brought more disciplinary cases to the notice of the Archbishop's court than any other clergyman in the area, he was nevertheless tender towards the offenders. He wrote to defend four women for not appearing at York and thus seeming to be in contempt of court. They had been excommunicated for 'not Seasonably acknowledging and making or performing publick penance for their Crimes of Fornication and Contumacy.' Grimshaw and his churchwardens signed a statement to the effect that the women were too poor to be able to pay the dues for their penance orders or their absolutions, and as they were truly penitent and heartily wanted to be readmitted into the church, they asked for leniency. Their request was granted.

An instance of public penance is provided in the case of Esther

Above: Beauty in decay at Heptonstall

Above: *The ruined church, Heptonstall*

Greenwood. The printed form that had to be filled in states that she must appear on a Sunday morning in the presence of the whole congregation. She had to be bareheaded, barefoot and barelegged, having a white sheet draped from the shoulders to her feet and a white wand in her hand. After the reading of the Gospel, she had to stand on a seat before the pulpit and recite after Grimshaw:

'Whereas, I good People, forgetting my duty to Almighty God have committed the Detestable Sin of Fornication with Joseph Wright (now a soldier) and thereby have justly provoked the heavy Wrath of God against me, to the great Danger of my own Soul, and evil Example of others, I do earnestly Repent, and am heartily Sorry for the same, desiring Almighty God for the Merits of Jesus Christ, to forgive me both this and all other my Offences, and also hereafter, so to assist me with his Holy Spirit, that I never fall into the like Offence again, and for that End and Purpose, I desire you all here Present, to pray with me, and for me, saying.

Our Father which art in Heaven ...'

Those who failed to do penance were excommunicated and publicly denounced. These punishments may seem harsh to us today, and in fact, they were already on their way out in Grimshaw's day—his own brother had joined the majority in not enforcing them—but Grimshaw only seems to have invoked this when private and public reproach had failed. These actions were 'visual aids' to help maintain order among a people who were mainly illiterate and wild.

Grimshaw was not just a prosecutor; he defended a parishioner from Stanbury who was on trial for forgery. If found guilty, the man would have been

Above: The font used by Grimshaw, now in the churchyard at Haworth

hanged, but Grimshaw demonstrated to the court's satisfaction that the man was actually illiterate. He also acted as Commissioner for Oaths and helped a number of people to write their wills.

Grimshaw extends his ministry

It might seem a small thing for Grimshaw to minister to the Darney Societies and those he himself had set up, but this meant he was extending his ministry into other parishes, and these boundaries were jealously guarded and also protected by church law. Although Grimshaw believed he should preach further afield without invitation, he confessed to a 'Nicodemial fear'. Like Nicodemus in the gospel story (John 3:1–21) he was afraid

to step out of line, perhaps because he was breaking ecclesiastical law and could lose his living as a clergyman. Nevertheless, he felt such a strong call from God that he overcame his fear. See map on page 86.

Grimshaw was quite tall but was so broad that he appeared stocky; he was full of energy, and when out on foot would often vault farm gates. His whole demeanour was resolute and confident of the gospel he had been charged to proclaim. But there was no arrogance about him, he knew enough about his own sin, especially his 'constitutional weakness' to protect him from that. His was the confidence founded on many hours alone with God in prayer.

William seems to have begun his itinerant work in 1747, first preaching in neighbouring parishes such as Leeds and Birstall, Todmorden, Shore and Rossendale. He was a member of the turnpike trust set up in 1735 to improve the road from Bradford through Haworth to Colne and contributed £100 to the cause; a very large sum of money, equal to about a year's salary. The trustees met about once a year, usually in the *Black Bull* and occasionally in *The King's Arms,* also in Haworth. Grimshaw and John Wesley used the improving road to visit the Colne area in 1747.

The vicar of Colne, George White, was often absent from his duties. He had trained for the Roman Catholic priesthood at Douai but then left and was accepted into holy orders in the Anglican church. He was a

Above: The walk to the church from 'Sowdens'

scholarly and aggressive man and often the worse for drink. One night on returning to his parish, he is said to have read the funeral service over twenty bodies that had been interred in his absence.

Grimshaw the praying preacher

Grimshaw's preaching and praying were both equally powerful in their effect on the large and small crowds he preached to. 'Dicky' Burdsall, who later became one of William's preachers, described first hearing him: 'When we got to the place (Eldwick), I trembled so much with the cold that I thought it would be impossible for me to bear it for long … After waiting for a short time, a broadset, sharp-looking little man appeared, habited as a layman, and buttoned up from the storm. Having quickly loosed his garments, in a moment he was in the pulpit and giving out a hymn the people sang like thunder. His voice in prayer seemed to me as it had been the voice of an angel. After prayer he took a little Bible out of his pocket, and read the following words for his text: "Glory to God in the highest, and on earth peace, good-will toward men." The Holy Ghost now shone upon my heart, and discovered to me that both myself and all mankind were in a lost and perishing condition while in a state of nature. I wept …'

John Newton, the converted slave-trader who himself became a mighty preacher and friend of Grimshaw, had an acquaintance who commented, 'I have often heard Mr. Grimshaw with great astonishment, and I hope with profit. In prayer … he excelled most men I have ever heard. His soul was carried out in that exercise with such earnestness, affection and fervour, as indicated the most intimate communion with God. His love and compassion for the souls of poor sinners, and his concern for their salvation, were manifested in the strongest manner in all his proceedings.'

Grimshaw began to see that the emotion that affected some of the hearers when he preached was not genuine and had to be curbed. He

Above: A commemorative stone at 'Sowdens' recalling some of those who stayed here in Grimshaw's time

Left: The 'new' church through the old at Heptonstall. John Wesley described the old church, which was finally destroyed by a storm in 1847, as the 'ugliest church' that he had ever seen

noticed, 'Soon after the devil observed such cryings and distress of soul, and agitation of body to affect people under the Word, he also began to seize people under the Word with strange unnatural distortions, convulsions, hideous roarings, to bring, as we plainly saw, contempt and disgrace upon the true work of God.' When he saw this happening, he would pause and ensure that these people calmed down and listened to the word or were ejected from the meeting. John and Charles Wesley also encountered and disallowed similar counterfeits in their own ministry.

News of the spiritual awakening in Haworth soon spread and attracted visitors of the calibre of Ingham, the Wesleys, and George Whitefield. Ingham initially stayed at the *Black Bull*, just outside the church gates, and run by Jonathan Whitehead, Grimshaw's parish clerk. It was not long before Ingham and Grimshaw became firm friends, as was the case with the other evangelists. In fact, 'Sowdens' became a centre for travelling evangelists, and one or two of the local preachers had a permanent home there. When the parsonage was full, Grimshaw would sleep in the barn and would often rise before his guests in the morning and be found cleaning their shoes. He kept an Alderney cow that provided enough milk for the household, but she would insist on following him down the hill to church so eventually he sold her.

Enemies of the revival

This new spiritual life in Haworth also provoked opposition. George White, the vicar at Colne, was a vehement opponent of the evangelicals and, when he was present in his parish would deal violently with the preachers. Similarly, Kennet, the vicar of Bradford, had not forgotten that he had scores to settle with the Haworth trustees and he disliked the attention the young minister of Haworth was attracting. Moves were being made behind the scenes to bring Grimshaw before the same ecclesiastical court that had banned Ingham from preaching in Yorkshire. Accusations were being laid that would require Grimshaw to give an account of his actions.

Grimshaw's vision

On Sunday 2 September 1744, less than a month after he had renewed his solemn covenant to God, William had an experience that made an indelible impression on his life. When his maid woke at five in the morning, she discovered the pastor was already at prayer. Shortly after, he left to hold a meeting at the house of a parishioner and on his return went immediately to his study to pray. Later that morning as he was reading the second lesson in the service, Grimshaw complained of feeling faint and asked Jonathan Whitehead, his clerk, to help him. Suddenly he collapsed at the reading desk but recovered after a short while and with help staggered out of the church. The faithful vicar thought he was dying and urged his bewildered congregation, with what strength he had, to prepare for their own death and trust in Christ alone for salvation. At the church door Grimshaw asked the congregation to remain where they were as he would soon return and share something extraordinary with them.

White and shaking, Grimshaw was taken to the parlour of the *Black Bull,* close by the church's main gate, where hot cloths were put on his arms and legs—which were 'as cold as death'—to restore the circulation. Grimshaw was conscious but sat motionless staring at the ceiling.

He later said that he had fallen into a trance and had seen and heard unforgettable things. He found himself at the entrance of a long dark foul passage, through which he understood he had to pass. High walls bound the passage on either side and on the right hand, beyond the wall, was heaven—beyond the left, was hell. As he groped his way through the dark passage, he heard a conversation between the Father and Jesus. God was saying that he couldn't save him because he was still trusting in his own efforts and had not cast himself wholeheartedly on Jesus. His future seemed very bleak. Then he heard Jesus pleading for him. There was a long pause while he

Above: The new church was completed in 1854 at Heptonstall

was left in suspense between hope and despair. Finally he saw the Lord Jesus Christ push his wounded hands and feet down through the ceiling. The nail holes were ragged and bluish with fresh blood streaming from them. Suddenly William was filled with joy and with a firm assurance that he was saved. Immediately his limbs warmed and he stood up. The maid thought he was in great rapture and this was confirmed by his words: 'I have had a glorious vision from the third heaven.' He said no more but went back into the church for the afternoon service that began at 2 pm—four hours after he had been taken ill. Grimshaw did not tell them of the vision he had seen, but he preached so long that it was 7 pm before the congregation dispersed.

This experience fundamentally affected Grimshaw's ministry. There was an increase in conversions both in Haworth and elsewhere and he was now doubly sure of his salvation, and only doubted it on occasions when in spite of great determination and pleading with God, he had succumbed again to his 'constitutional weakness'. The experience of this vision would be something he would recall with gratitude for the grace of God in reaching him in such a remarkable and personal way and it was of such an intimate nature that he could not share it until much later and then only to a select few. Joseph Williams, a nonconformist clothier from Kidderminster who often visited Haworth, was a confidante of Grimshaw's and preserved this account.

Grimshaw marvelled at the ways of God, particularly noting that no two conversions were alike: 'There are not two in every five hundred that are born again

Above: The Chantry House at Heptonstall—formerly used as a charnel house where bones were stored

or brought in Christ, every way alike.' Joseph Williams commented, 'He observes there is such a diversity in the Spirit's operations, that scarce any two of them have been wrought upon in the same way. Some have sunk down in the church under a terrifying sense of divine wrath, while others have been drawn with the cords of love. Some have received a sealed pardon in a few weeks or days, while others have been held many months under a spirit of bondage.'

The workload of the busy pastor became so heavy that he began to enlist the help of laymen to preach the gospel, a practice he was later to find had also been adopted by the Wesleys. Scotch Will was probably the first layman he used, particularly as he had heard him and been blessed by him, but there were also John Wilkinson, Thomas Colbeck, Thomas Mitchell and others. More laymen were enrolled in his area than in any other circuit in the country. However, his generous spirit claimed that as many had been converted under them as under his own ministry.

Some of these laymen lived at 'Sowdens' while others found it a place of refreshment, training and encouragement. Although he encouraged the evangelists to preach to each other at 'Sowdens', as a way of training them, the best preparation they could receive would be to model themselves on their godly leader. His humility, prayerfulness, and boundless energy would be an encouragement to them all.

Heptonstall

OS Grid reference SD 980281

Heptonstall is an ancient settlement perched high in the Pennines. Its name is from the Old English *Hep, 'wild rose'* and *Tunstall*, 'cattle farm', although the land here has never been good enough solely for farming. The Romans are thought to have had a camp here. Paulinus (d. AD 644) the first Archbishop of York preached here on his mission to convert King Edwin and his subjects to Christ. Surprisingly there is no mention of the town in the Domesday Book,

even though there was a manor here that William the Conqueror gave to his compatriot Earl Warren. Pack horse trains used to bring large quantities of lime to make the ground more fertile but it was not enough to support the community so they also based their economy on hand-loom weaving. In the last years of the 18th century the population was 4,000, double what it is now, but the construction of the Rochdale Canal drained the valley bottom and provided a transport route for coal, and the trade moved down to steam-powered mills in Hebden Bridge leaving Heptonstall well preserved.

Above: Here lies David Hartley, the 'King of the Coiners'

Churches and Churchyard

It is very rare to have two churches in one churchyard. The old church, dedicated to God and St Thomas, was said by John Wesley to be the ugliest church he knew. The west face of the tower fell away in the great storm of 1847 and was not rebuilt. The new church was completed in 1854. There are said to be 100,000 bodies in the churchyard. Some gravestones have been used more than once with one set of inscriptions

face down to the soil. One stone near the altar of the ruined church is in memory of 'MRS Grace Cockroft…who died UNMARRIED in 1745.' Another is of David Hartley, 'King' of the Cragg Vale Coiners hanged in 1770 for 'unlawfully stamping and clipping a public coin.' This can be found by counting 12 stone slabs forward from the porch of the old church then two down to the left.

Above: The 'old' church at Heptonstall

The Heptonstall Octagon

John Wesley preached in 'the shell of the New House at Heptonstall' on 5 July 1764. Because of their association with Grimshaw, the Wesleys came frequently, John twenty-one times and Charles quite often. The octagonal shape was chosen to avoid conflict with the established church and John Wesley wished all his preaching houses could be this shape. Earlier ones were built at Norwich (1757), Rotherham (1761) and Whitby (1762); ten others were erected after the one here.

Heptonstall by car

From Todmorden east on A646 for just under 5 mi, then turn left on minor roads for a further 2 mi, total 7 mi (12 km)

From Halifax west on A646 for 8 mi then take turning circle and left on minor roads for a further 2 mi, total 10 mi (16 km)

Above: Heptonstall Moor

Top: Heptonstall Octagon

Heptonstall by bus

Route H2 from Hebden Bridge, or 500 from Halifax or Hebden Bridge.

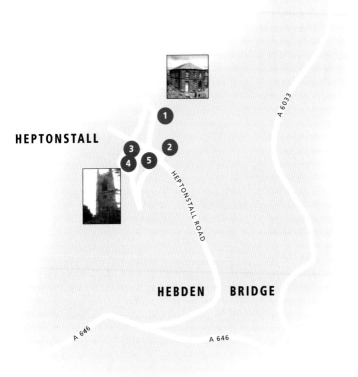

PECKET WELL

HEPTONSTALL

HEPTONSTALL ROAD

A 6033

HEBDEN BRIDGE

A 646

A 646

KEY TO PLACES

1 METHODIST OCTAGON CHURCH

2 LITHERSTONE

3 OLD CHURCH RUINS

4 ST THOMAS'S CHURCH

5 GRAMMAR SCHOOL MUSEUM

⑤ The message spreads

To add to the sadness of the loss of his second wife, Grimshaw's enemies increased their efforts to silence him when he made contact with the despised Methodists.

On 22 October 1746 when Charles Wesley first visited Haworth, at the suggestion of Colbeck and Wilkinson, both William and Elizabeth were ill in bed with the high fever typical of the 'plague' that regularly ravaged Haworth. No doubt Grimshaw, who would not desert his pastoral duties on any pretext, had caught it while visiting his parishioners. Charles wrote in his diary: 'She (Elizabeth) had been a great opposer, but lately convinced. His soul was full of triumphant love … We prayed, believing that the Lord would raise him up again for the service of His Church.' On this occasion, Charles preached somewhere in the village and his text was from Isaiah 35.

Sadly, Elizabeth died from the fever. Although an obvious shock, her loss did not affect Grimshaw as severely as the loss of Sarah, perhaps because for so long she had been an 'opposer' and so must have made his busy life difficult for him. The relationship does not appear to have been as close as that with Sarah. Also, during this period, he had probably been revising his opinions about marriage. He was later to write: 'Christians are like apprentices, they must serve Christ seven years

Above: *The packhorse trail that the cortege of Elizabeth Grimshaw would have taken in 1746*

Facing page: *Todmorden Edge Farm— now a private house—where the first Methodist quarterly meeting was held on 18 October 1748*

before one can confide in them'—and he did not think that they should marry during their 'apprenticeship'. He added that: 'Believers' souls seldom prosper who marry in the youth of grace … domestic necessaries and then the increase of their family … so divert their minds from their souls … that they are long before, if ever, they recover themselves again. These, I suppose, live and die at best but babes in Christ. Therefore, it is most advisable that God's people should abstain from marriage, 'til they are grown strong and are established in grace … 'Tis certainly a device of Satan to get young, inexperienced believers entangled with one another, and to persuade them that such engagements are of God.' It all sounds like lessons from hard experience!

The funeral procession for Elizabeth wound its way over the moorland track to her family church at Heptonstall. As with Sarah's funeral, the coffin would be swung between two black-plumed horses, and the mourners rode or walked behind. Whatever William's feelings for Elizabeth, he did not alter his intention to be buried as near as Sarah as possible. He did contemplate a further marriage about twelve years after Elizabeth's death, and for guidance, used a method favoured by Benjamin Ingham and the Moravians, and that John Wesley once used—he prayed about the matter, tossed a gold coin and received guidance not to marry again!

The loss of Elizabeth also posed problems for the care of Sarah's children, John and Jane. Although Molly his housekeeper was probably in the household at that time, they would be likely to spend more time than ever at their Grandfather Lockwood's. The fact that John had named them as

Above: *The Octagon from the Haworth packhorse trail. To the left is the old Sunday School (1891)*

Above: Todmorden Edge Farm

virtually sole beneficiaries of his estate indicates that there was a strong bond between them.

Grimshaw becomes a Methodist

Charles Wesley returned to Haworth three months after he had first visited and Grimshaw invited him to stay at 'Sowdens' though he did not offer the church to him as he had heard derogatory rumours about the Wesleys. So Charles preached in a large house that was not big enough to accommodate his hearers. He then visited the Darney societies—Will had decided he could no longer supervise them.

Before he left, Charles told Grimshaw that he should not have been afraid to lend him his pulpit as it would have been quite lawful for him to do so, and William was ashamed at having been influenced by the enemies of the gospel. Regardless of this affront

to Charles, they developed a warm friendship that remained strong in spite of Grimshaw's resolute defence of Scotch Will against the Wesleys' reluctance to recognise him as one of their preachers. Charles visited again a few days later and was offered the Darney societies. Later in the year, May 1747, John Wesley visited for the first time and inspected those societies. This time the Methodist evangelist was invited to preach from Grimshaw's pulpit. From now on Grimshaw wholeheartedly joined himself to the Methodists although, like the Wesleys, he continued to consider himself a loyal member of the Church of England.

Soon after John's visit, William wrote to him offering to add to his parish duties visits to the Darney societies and others in the area: 'As my own convenience will permit, and their circumstances may respectively require.' He also

Above: *Moorland track, a scene familiar to Grimshaw in his parish visiting and beyond*

said that he wanted to work in harmony with the Wesleys and hoped for a free and open communication with them in future. He added, 'My pulpit, I hope, shall be always at yours and your brother's service, and my house, so long as I have one, your welcome home. The same I'll make it to all our fellow-labourers, through the grace of God.'

Examining believers

William Grimshaw took his visits to the societies very seriously. It was not enough for members to attend, they had to show they were growing in grace and to this end he would 'examine' each member individually. This was probably based on his own practice of examining himself which he described in this way: 'The more I look inward and search into the state of my own soul or the more I converse with others about the spiritual state of their souls, the more I experience the ways of the Holy Spirit in and with the children of God. Hence it is evident to me that we can never enough exceed in self-examination and spiritual communion and society. Self-examination and meditation are mighty helps in prayer … we should always use both before prayer … I find that reading and hearing the Word of God is good, but I experience that private prayer, heart or self-examination, meditation and contemplation is far better … such Christians as read much but meditate, examine etc little are generally though wise and notional, barren, cold and lifeless … but the others are lively and fervent.' He said his ideal was that for every hour spent reading he would spend five in prayer, meditation and self-examination.

Above: The moorland trails are still well-used—but now for leisure pursuits

Grimshaw loved his fellow Christians and we can be sure that, threatening though the practice of examination sounds; he would deal tenderly with the class members and encourage them in their commitment. Moreover, this practice was based on his own which, as we have seen, he knew to be very beneficial. People are said to have walked twenty miles over the moorland hills to hear Grimshaw and he himself was not averse to walking a similar distance to preach even to a small group, although when he was visiting his 'round' he would take his horse.

Grimshaw had a mischievous sense of humour. When he arrived as a visiting preacher at one church, the churchwarden mentioned that the congregation was not keen on long sermons and even when Mr Wesley came, he never preached for more than an hour. William replied, 'Mr Wesley, God bless him, can do as much in an hour as I can in two!'

Methodists under suspicion

All this activity was undertaken against a background of civil unrest in the country. In 1745 the Jacobite rebels from Scotland had marched relatively unopposed through northern England and were at Pendle Forest not far away. The Methodists were accused of being their supporters, which was clearly not the case since Jacobite support came largely from the Roman Catholics, and in fact Grimshaw had become a recruiting officer for the king's army. Darney's Scottish accent put him under suspicion and his society at Miller Barn was attacked. Added to this, there was anxiety about the wool trade as the Jacobites had cut one of their transport routes into Lancashire.

It was likely that the invading army would come into Yorkshire to attack General Wade's army garrisoned at York. If they did so, Haworth and its surrounding area would be on their route and there could be fierce fighting and severe loss as the army plundered for supplies. As it happened, the army moved down the west of the country at speed finding little opposition but also failing to provoke the expected rising of the people in their favour. Reaching Derby, they halted and retreated back to Scotland. Evidence now suggests they could have taken London.

The Sacrament at Haworth

Although he was renowned for his preaching, observing the proper liturgical procedures was important to Grimshaw and especially the observance of Holy Communion: 'Sacrament receiving must be daily, diligently, and devoutly observed … Means of grace and duties can never have too much of our diligence; nor too little of our dependence.' Shockingly for the time Grimshaw was using laymen to preach, but still he would not allow them to administer Holy Communion. Like the Wesleys, a 'high churchman' in his views, he advocated that Methodists should accept the elements even from a worldly priest's hands as his worldliness would not affect a sacrament received in faith. Taken in faith, the bread and wine became flesh and blood to the believer's soul as much as the bread and wine became food for

Lay Preachers in Guiseley: an account by Thomas Mitchell

One evening while William Darney was preaching, the curate of Guiseley came at the head of a large mob, who threw eggs in his face, pulled him down, dragged him out of the house on the ground, and stamped on him … Some time after, Jonathan Maskew came. As soon as he began to speak, the same mob came, pulled him down, and dragged him out of the house. They then tore off his clothes, and dragged him along upon his naked back over the gravel and pavement. When they thought they had sufficiently bruised him, they let him go … With much difficulty, he crept to a friend's house, where they dressed his wounds, and got him some clothes. It was my turn to go next. No sooner was I at the town, than the mob came, like so many roaring lions. My friends advised me not to preach that night; and undertook to carry me out of the town. But the mob followed me in a great rage, and stoned me for near two miles, so that it was several weeks before I got well of the bruises. About this time, a carpenter was swearing horribly, whom I calmly reproved. He immediately flew in a violent passion, and having an axe … swore he would cleave my head … but just as he was going to strike, a man … snatched hold of his arm, and held him till his passion cooled. At first, I felt a little fear, but it soon vanished away.'

the body. Early Methodists would normally go to church in the morning, where they might receive the Sacrament, and then go to the preaching house where they would receive Methodist teaching. The intention was never to be an alternative to the Established Church.

Communion services were an uplifting experience at Haworth. Grimshaw chose relevant hymns which he sang with a strength of voice that 'seemed more than mortal' and he would divert from the set order to give 'pious and animating exhortations'. With over a thousand communicants at times, Grimshaw bought two flagons to meet the need for wine. William would conduct the first service at 9 am and would preach in it; the congregation would then file out of the church to make room for the next communicants and the services would continue until the need had been met. Those who left the church would remain to have fellowship in the churchyard and, if there was a visiting preacher would hear a further sermon there. It was said that the people enjoyed a heaven on earth and made their way home full of joy and praise.

In spite of their determination to remain faithful to the Anglican church, it was the priests of that church who were the most antagonistic to these Methodists. Often they would incite mob violence against the preachers. Although clergy such as Grimshaw and the Wesleys were assaulted, the laymen bore the brunt of the violence.

Grimshaw's ecclesiastical trials

When Archbishop Herring, a radically inclined man dubbed 'Red Herring', retired from York in 1747, Grimshaw's enemies struck. Herring had been generally tolerant of the new movement and so they had to wait for his successor. The details are unclear but charges were laid against Grimshaw, probably by his own vicar, Kennet, that he was neglecting his parish and had been preaching in non-conformist licensed preaching houses. Grimshaw's friend Ingham had been disciplined by this court and another friend had been dismissed from his ministry due to his preaching the Gospel, so

Above: Grimshaw provided two of these flagons for Holy Communion

Above: *Guiseley parish church—where the curate organised beatings of the evangelicals*

Grimshaw had cause to be anxious. He was called to face the charges at Wakefield on 25 May 1748 where Archbishop Hutton asked him how many communicants he had in the parish when he started. 'Twelve, my Lord.' 'And how many now?' 'In the winter from four to five hundred, and sometimes in the summer near twelve hundred.' Hutton dismissed the charge saying, 'We cannot find fault with Mr Grimshaw as he is instrumental in bringing such numbers to the Lord's Table.'

He may still have been dismissed if it could have been proved that he had been preaching in dissenters' licensed buildings. Fortunately, he had not done so, and he was acquitted on the promise that he would never preach in such a building. However, no restriction was placed on him regarding preaching in the open air or in private houses. Grimshaw, who habitually spent a lot of time in praise, would have overflowed with it on his way home.

Some years later, his enemies again complained to a new Archbishop. John Gilbert arrived at Haworth for a confirmation service with a retinue of clergy, some of whom had instigated the visit. He had a word with Grimshaw in private, discussing some of the complaints, one of which was that his sermons were very loose and he could and did preach about everything. The Archbishop gave him a text and said that he wished to hear him preach on it in two hours' time.

Above: An engine takes on water at Haworth

Grimshaw is reported to have looked out of the vestry door and seeing an expectant crowd asked why they should have to wait for two hours. He went into the church, prayed fervent extempore prayers for the Archbishop and launched into his sermon. After the people had left, the clergy waited to hear the verdict. Hutton took Grimshaw by the arm and with a tremor in his voice said, 'I wish to God that all the clergy in my diocese were like this good man.'

Later, speaking to friends at 'Sowdens', Grimshaw declared, 'I did expect to be turned out of my parish on this occasion, but if I had, I would have joined my friend Wesley, taken my saddle bags and gone to one of the poorest circuits.'

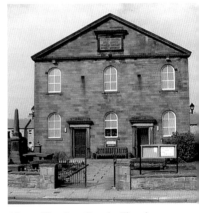

Above: West Lane Baptist Church, Haworth. James Hartley, who was converted under Grimshaw's ministry, formed what is now the West Lane Baptist Church with a group of Methodists in 1748. He became their first pastor. Constructed in 1752, the building was enlarged in 1775

Visit Haworth by rail

The Keighley and Worth Valley Railway, a preserved line using steam engines and vintage diesels runs every weekend and school holidays and almost every day from July to August. This is the line that was used for the filming of *The Railway Children* and there is a walk associated with that from Oakworth to Haworth and Oxenhope. There are six stations. At Keighley there is a direct connection to the national rail network, a turntable and souvenir kiosk. Ingrow West has the Museum of Rail Travel. Damens is Britain's smallest railway station. Oakworth station, entirely lit by gas, is the one featured in the 1970 film. Haworth station has a railway shop that is open all the year round. Oxenhope at the end of the line has a station shop and buffet car.

It is a very steep walk over the footbridge from Haworth station to the

The Railway Children

This is a children's story written by Edith Nesbit in 1906 that draws on similar experiences in her own life. The story concerned an upper middle class family where the father worked for the English Foreign Office and one night was mysteriously taken away by officials. Mother says he is 'working away' but his absence means that the family have to move from their large house to a much smaller one in the countryside. As mother cannot afford to send them to school they spend much of their time near the local railway and have various adventures, the story culminates with the father's happy return. There were serialised BBC Television productions of the story in 1951 and 1957, a film directed by Lionel Jeffries in 1970, and a Carlton Television film in 2000. Jenny Agutter played the eldest child 'Bobbie' in the 1970 film and her mother in the later production. It is the 1970 film that was shot on the Keighley and Worth Valley Railway, and the Brontë Parsonage is used as one of the houses.

main places of interest in Haworth. You can catch bus services 663, 664, 665 and 720 from opposite the station to take you up the hill.

Haworth station ☎ 01535 645214

24 hour information line ☎ 01535 647777

www.kwvr.co.uk

The Cobbled Way café in Main Street is small but has a large menu. Open from 1000–1700. ☎ 01535 642 735

The *Black Bull* in Main Street serves meals all day and has overnight accommodation. ☎ 01535 642249

Chaplin's Bistro in Oak Street, near the railway station, is open 1700–2200 Tuesday—Saturday and 1200–2100 Sunday. ☎ 01535 648090

The *Robin Hood Inn* at Pecket Well (once Becket's Well) on the A6033 is a

17th century coaching inn four miles from Haworth and 1 mile from Hebden Bridge. Food is served all day and there is overnight accommodation. ☎ 01422 842593 www.robinhoodsinn.com

Facing page: KWVR entrance hall Keighley

Top of page: *Waiting for the train at Haworth*

Above: *Train arrives at Haworth*

⑥ Pulling the devil's teeth

A man of strong character and ceaseless action, Grimshaw drove himself to the limit in his passion to preach Christ—and he expected all Christians to follow his lead. Those who did, frequently bore the scars of battle

It was not always peaceable at 'Sowdens' and at times there could be heated theological debates. Of the two who were called 'Grimshaw's men', Paul Greenwood believed that salvation was open to all, and Jonathan Maskew believed that only those who had been elected could be saved. Grimshaw saw his role as keeping the balance between the two as evenly as possible. Although he was more in sympathy with Maskew's view, he felt the important thing was not to argue about doctrine but to preach the gospel and this was what both his men did well. Winning souls for Jesus, he said, was like pulling the devil's teeth.

One of the doctrines of the Methodists was that a Christian could be completely sinless (see the box in *Travel with William Booth* p.71 in this series). Grimshaw disagreed strongly with this position because that was not at all his experience—William was well aware of his inability to lead a sinless life. He wrote, 'In a regenerate state, two corruptions chiefly plague us and cost us more pain than all to subdue. The one is our constitutional sin, which we

Above: The Road Ahead—one of the tracks on Penistone Hill

Facing page: The church at Luddenden

Above: The Stocks at Midgley which Grimshaw would have seen in use

Facing page: View from Ewood in Midgley

used to be most addicted to in nature… the other one is lust, consequently he whose constitutional infirmity is the latter has but that to struggle with.' This appears to set out clearly his experience. He said young believers tend to look too much to their temptations and too little at their peace: 'But old believers in the strongest and longest temptations always eye their peace and by this mercy even in the roughest trials are always composed, steady and happy.' But even mature believers are never free of sin: 'The best believer, if he knows what he says, and says the truth, is but a sinner at best.'

After Elizabeth's death, Grimshaw spent a good deal of time at Ewood with the children. He wrote from there to tell John Wesley that, 'This evening I am venturing, by the divine

Mr Grimshaw's men

Paul Greenwood, a tall, thin, dark-haired man from Ponden Hall near Haworth, went into the family barn to pray under deep conviction of sin. His father, anxious because of his long absence, approached the barn to see if he was all right. He saw Paul kneeling and then joined him in prayer. The mother then went looking for the pair—then a brother and a sister and they all ended up in the barn pleading for mercy and before they left had each found peace with God. Paul became one of the best-loved preachers, of similar temperament to Grimshaw himself. John Pawson described him as: 'A truly apostolical man, and exceedingly beloved by the people … one of the most sincere and upright men I was ever acquainted with.'

Jonathan Maskew's Quaker father turned him out of his home in the corn mill in Burley-in-Wharfedale when he became a Methodist. Grimshaw invited him to 'Sowdens' and he lived there as William's manservant but he also became a powerful preacher. Maskew took life very seriously, so much so that nobody could remember hearing him laugh, but when he spoke of Christ it was with genuine warmth. He often used to exclaim from the pulpit: 'Oh that name Jesus! How sweet it is!'

assistance, upon a public exhortation in a wild, unchristian place, called Midgley … where of late I have a great part of my residence.'

Perhaps Grimshaw was at Ewood when John Lockwood died aged eighty and was laid to rest at Luddenden. No doubt attending another funeral at the church where Sarah was buried brought back painful memories for him. Although no mention is made of them, John (9) and Jane (8) would greatly miss their granddad. The children probably stayed on in the house they were due to inherit as they would know the servants and be at home there. This could only be a temporary measure, however, because Grimshaw would wish them to have a good schooling.

Alternating between Ewood and Haworth did not diminish Grimshaw's activities elsewhere; he still committed himself wholeheartedly to the work of God. He was building up a good band of preachers and a regular circuit of societies to teach and

Above: The Lord Nelson, opposite the church gate, was a private house in Grimshaw's time, but when Branwell Brontë was stationmaster at Luddenden, he often drank here. The station has long gone

Above: High Street Pateley Bridge

Facing page: The River Nidd at the foot of High Street where Tommy Lee was thrown into the water

examine in Yorkshire and Lancashire. In addition, he had also started the first Methodist Quarterly meeting at Todmorden Edge Farm. His prayer was that, 'I may prove faithful and indefatigable in his vineyard! That I may persevere to the last gasp, steadfast, immovable, always abounding in his work!' Grimshaw always felt he would have a short life and therefore had to use it to the full for the Lord: 'By the grace of God, I'm resolved never to flag while I can ride, creep or crawl.' He had no desire: 'To go creeping to heaven at last.' Some might say that his hectic lifestyle was such as to guarantee a short life. A few years before his death, he said that he was in continual pain—but he continued to persevere.

He once tenderly wrote to Thomas Lee, one of his preachers:

Tommy Lee at Pateley Bridge

In writing his life story, Tommy records what happened at Pateley Bridge: 'The first time I was there Mr—— had prepared and encouraged a numerous mob, who spared neither mud nor stones with many strokes besides, so that they themselves owned: "We have done enough to make an end of him." I did, indeed, reel to and fro, and my head was broken with a stone. But I never found my soul more happy, nor was ever more composed in my closet. It was a glorious time; and there are several who date their conversion from (then). The malice of the devil was levelled against me, as I was the first that disturbed his servants in those parts … carrying as it were my life in my hand. One day, as I was going through Pateley, the captain of the mob, who was kept in constant pay, pursued me, and pulled me off my horse. The mob then soon collected about me; and one or other struck up my heels (I believe more than twenty times) upon the stones. They then dragged me into a house by the hair of the head; then pushed me back, with one or two upon me, and threw me with the small of my back upon the edge of the stone stairs. This nearly broke my back; and it was not well for many years after. Thence they dragged me to the bridge and threw me into the water.' Tommy died thirty-five years later aged sixty having gone to preach twice that day on crutches.

'I hope that you can preach twenty times a week. If you can preach oftener, do. Preaching is health, food and physic to me, and why not to thee, my brother. Besides, Tommy, there is very great need of preaching now, for iniquity aboundeth, the love of many grows cold and God's judgements are out in the earth. Tommy, let us preach four times a day or thirty times a week, whichever you please or can better bear. Our Master well deserves it. Yea, and infinitely more.' He was not asking Lee to do more than he did himself, and his sermons were often two hours long because he

Above: Helmsley Castle

didn't wish to leave anything out for fear some would miss the word they needed.

Grimshaw allowed nothing to stop him fulfilling his preaching rounds. One day after walking fifteen miles and preaching, he came to a swollen river that he had expected to cross on stepping stones. He waded through the river, arrived at the preaching house on time and preached in wet clothes before starting his journey back. He expected ordinary Christians to make sacrifices too. He believed they should go to the meeting regardless of the weather because even if they stayed at home and prayed they would not receive the same kind of blessing.

Driving the wife to church

However, although he did drive reluctant parishioners with a whip, he would not have recommended the following practice: A Quaker who lived six miles from Haworth went to hear Grimshaw out of curiosity. He was converted and tried to persuade his wife to go with him to the church. She responded, 'I'll not go to hear that black devil.' He tried to reason with her but she remained adamant. Finally he forced her to dress in her Sunday best, took a rod and drove her—as if he was taking a beast to market—all the way to Haworth. Throughout the 'march', she shouted abuse about Grimshaw. The following Sunday, she went to church of her own accord and was challenged throughout the service. Grimshaw sought her out afterwards and made an appointment to preach in their home. She was converted and their farmhouse became one of his earliest preaching centres.

William alternated between 'quiet' weeks when he would

preach about fifteen times, and 'busy' weeks, preaching as far away as Helmsley, Osmotherly and Newcastle (113 miles—181 kilometres) in the east and Preston, Ingleton and Kendal (56 miles—90 kilometres) in the west, although most of his activities were confined within a circle of fifteen miles around Haworth.

William Darney visited Grimshaw's circuit too although not in such a planned way. He set up a thriving group in Heptonstall where the 'octagonal' chapel was built with Thomas Colbeck's money. There was already an octagon in Rotherham where the roof for the Heptonstall chapel was made and transported over the hills—an early example of prefabrication. It is no longer strictly octagonal as it had to be enlarged, but it does claim to be the oldest Methodist chapel that has been in regular use. Darney also preached in Scotland and Cornwall.

Above: End of the Packhorse Trail Heptonstall, a track Grimshaw would have covered many times

The urgency of winning souls

Grimshaw was a passionate evangelist and the way he inspired his fellow workers, and perhaps his style of preaching, can be seen in his unpublished notes *The Admonition of a Sinner.* Here he desired that we should set about winning others: 'Immediately— delay is dangerous. Consider the deplorable condition our poor ignorant fellow creatures are in— the longer the delay worse it grows—their sins increase, their evil habits grow stronger, their hearts are more hardened—their consciences more seared: the devil rules in them and rejoices; Christ

Above: Remains of Heptonstall stocks—once sited near The Cross Inn—churchwardens had the power to put people in the stocks for punishment

is excluded, the Holy Spirit rejected, God is continually dishonoured, his laws transgressed and his wrath provoked. Moreover, their time is wasting, their day of grace shortening and death and judgement approaching.'

He continued by stating his conviction that failure to seek to win others to Christ has disastrous consequences: 'We take the devil's part in destroying souls … Our connivance at the ways of the wicked is tacit approbation of Satan's destruction of them—if we are silent, we consent; if we are not against him we are for him—if we oppose him not we assist him and non-resistance of the devil in this case is doing half his work for him—O Shocking!' He contended that it is possible that we grieve the holy angels and: 'This sinful forbearance may impute many bodily afflictions and worldly losses. Various troubles may befall our families also.'

Scotch Will needed no encouragement, because at times he became too enthusiastic. However, he would insist on preaching that only those whom God had elected could come to Christ. This was a doctrine the Wesleys opposed, and Grimshaw had said there was no need to preach it in evangelism. He applied to be accepted as a Methodist itinerant preacher and was reluctantly accepted because of Grimshaw's support, but it needed frequent intervention by Grimshaw for him to continue in their number. On one occasion when Charles Wesley invited a number of preachers to meet him in Leeds, Darney turned up uninvited and they would not let him in. He also persisted in publishing his poems which were pure doggerel. Each time the

Wesleys gave him another chance, because of Grimshaw's support, but they insisted that he should stop: 'railing, begging and printing nonsense.' Nevertheless, he was a mighty evangelist who suffered a great deal of violence for his preaching.

Thousands hear the gospel at Haworth

When Charles Wesley revisited Haworth in January 1747, he said he had never seen a church better filled. After he had prayed in the pulpit the crowd outside complained that they could not hear him and begged him to come out. Charles stepped up on a tombstone and 'Between three and four thousand heard me gladly.' The crowd was standing on the graves, walls and roofs of the neighbouring houses—some even on the church roof or clinging to the tower. Wesley commented, 'The church leads [lead sealing the joins on the roof] and steeple were filled with clusters of people and all as still as night. If ever I

Facing page, top: Inside the Heptonstall Octagon opened the year after Grimshaw's death

Facing page, centre: Tribute to Scotch Will at Heptonstall Methodist Chapel—the oldest Methodist chapel in the world in continuous use

Top The middle house, Litherstone, was known as The Preaching House; Grimshaw and his helpers held meetings here from 1750 until the Octagon was built, and preachers often stayed here and may have spoken to the crowds from the upstairs windows

***Above:** Part of High Street Pateley Bridge*

preached the Gospel, I preached it then. The Lord take all the glory.'

George Whitefield, an eloquent and impassioned evangelist, preached to a crowded graveyard at Haworth on so many occasions that the platform and scaffolding outside the south wall became known as Whitefield's pulpit. On one awesome occasion, when the Countess of Huntingdon, a faithful supporter of evangelists, was present, he announced the text: 'It is appointed unto man once to die but after this the judgement.' He paused, there was a shriek and someone dropped dead! This was followed by a commotion and Whitefield motioned the audience to stay quiet. Grimshaw was then heard to say, 'Brother Whitefield, you stand among the dead and dying. An immortal soul has been called into eternity; the destroying angel is passing over the congregation:

cry aloud and spare not!' Whitefield announced the text again, there was another shriek and a person near to the Countess of Huntingdon died. The Countess begged Whitefield not to announce the text again.

On another occasion, Whitefield implied that the people of Haworth should know the Gospel. Grimshaw shouted out to the preacher: 'Oh sir! For God's sake, do not speak so! I pray you do not flatter them! I fear the greater part of them are going to hell with their eyes open.' Grimshaw and Whitefield were great friends, Grimshaw once assured him that as long as he had a shilling there would be sixpence for Whitefield.

Although the large crowds were coming to Haworth, Grimshaw was still happy to do personal evangelism. He distributed tracts and wrote at least one himself. Joseph Jones who lodged with him for some time said that, 'He used great plainness and simplicity in his conversation with all men, sparing neither poor nor rich, but boldly reproving all as necessity required.' Lord Huntingdon, the Countess' son who clearly did not share his mother's strong evangelical faith, had been involved in various arguments with eminent clergymen. He tried it with Grimshaw and received the rebuke: 'My Lord, if you need information, I would gladly do my utmost to assist you; but the fault is not in your head, but in your heart, which can only be reached by divine power.'

Above: *Nidderdale Museum*

Left: *Scene in the Nidderdale Museum*

TRAVEL INFORMATION

Pateley Bridge

OS grid reference SE 159658

By road

On the B6265 between Ripon and Skipton

Pateley Bridge is a small town set around a steep hill and is the main crossing of the river Nidd. Earlier prosperity was built on lead mining, quarrying and flax. England's oldest sweet shop is here. It was established in 1827, its timbers and beams come from one of Henry VIII's warships and the cash till dates from the 1850's. The Nidderdale Way 53 mi (83 km) starts and finishes in the High Street, looping round the river and affording spectacular views. There is a camping and caravanning site (☎ 01423 711383), glassblowers, pottery and the Nidderdale Museum.

The award-winning **Nidderdale Museum** occupies the original Victorian workhouse. Some of its displays are: a cobbler's store, general store, Victorian parlour, kitchen, schoolroom, chemist's, haberdashers, joiner's shop and solicitor's office. There are also agricultural and transport displays. Open 1400–1700 daily Easter—October; weekends only in winter months, ☎ 01423 711225

GRIMSHAW'S 'PARISH'

M 6
J 30
M 65
J 26
M 6
M 62
M 62
M 606
A 1
A 1 (M)
A 1

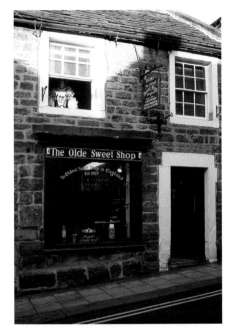

KEY TO PLACES

1 BRINDLE
2 ROUGHLEE
3 BARROWFORD
4 COLNE
5 TODMORDEN
6 HEPTONSTALL
7 HEBDEN BRIDGE
8 HAWORTH
9 KEIGHLEY
10 BRADFORD
11 GUISELEY
12 PATELEY BRIDGE
13 MOUNT GRACE PRIORY
14 OSMOTHERLEY
15 RIEVAULX ABBEY
16 HELMSLEY

Above: Tucked away in the picturesque village of
Pateley Bridge is the oldest sweet shop in England

Above: East Tower of Helmsley Castle

Above: Castle entrance

Helmsley

OS Grid reference SE 611836

Helmsley is a compact market town. Grimshaw preached here, probably in the market place at first. He would also have preached in the parish church where Dr Richard Conyers also began preaching the gospel some years after he started there in 1755. There is a record of Grimshaw's visit to him in November 1762. An old cross stands in the square and a market is held on Fridays. *The Black Swan* overlooks the market square and is an old inn with parts dating from Tudor, Elizabethan and Georgian periods. William Wordsworth stayed here. There are other inns, restaurants and cafes close to the square.

Helmsley Castle dates from the early 13th century and the ruins are surrounded by a ditch cut out of solid rock. The castle was owned by the Duke of Gloucester, who later became Richard III, from 1478–1485. It was rendered indefensible by the Parliamentary army after they defeated the Royalists there in 1644.

Open April to September 1000–1800; October to March 1000–1700; November to

This small town is popular with tourists and has many eating places: a fish and chip shop, two Indian restaurants and two cafes in the High Street. On Park Road, just off the High Street the *Willow Restaurant* ☎ 01423 711689 sells English meals and sandwiches. It also has en-suite accommodation.

Top: Fourteenth century hall, at Helmsley Castle

Above: Rievaulx Abbey

March Wednesday to Sunday 1000–1600. ☎ 01439 748283 www.theheritagetrail.co.uk/castles/helmsley%20castle.html

The Walled Garden, near the castle, dates from 1756 and has 150 varieties of clematis. Open April to October 1030–1700. ☎ 01439 771427. www.helmsleywalledgarden.co.uk

Rievaulx Abbey

Rievaulx Abbey is a majestic ruin with most of the 13th century church still standing and many outbuildings reaching a good height. The third Abbot, St Aelred's words still apply: 'Everywhere peace, everywhere serenity, and a marvellous freedom from the world.'

Open all year round

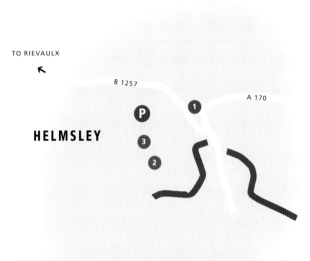

TO RIEVAULX

B 1257

A 170

P

1

3

2

HELMSLEY

KEY TO PLACES

1   THE BLACK SWAN AND MARKET PLACE

2   CASTLE (REMAINS OF)

3   WALLED GARDEN

Above: *Market place, Helmsley, where Grimshaw preached*

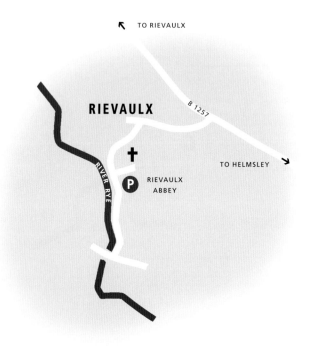

TO RIEVAULX

RIEVAULX

B 1257

RIVER RYE

TO HELMSLEY

✝

P RIEVAULX
ABBEY

Above: *Rievaulx Abbey*

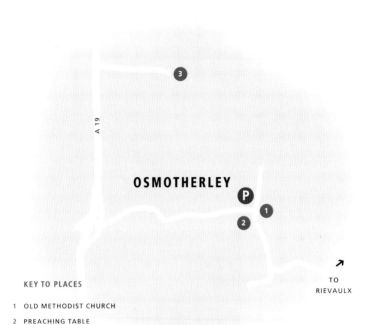

OSMOTHERLEY

A 19

P

TO
RIEVAULX

KEY TO PLACES

1 OLD METHODIST CHURCH

2 PREACHING TABLE

3 MOUNT GRACE PRIORY

Above: Monk's cell in Mount Grace Priory

except December 25, 26 and January 1. ☎ 01439 798228

Rievaulx Terrace and Temples stand on higher ground than the Abbey and have good views of it. Open 2nd March to 3rd November daily. ☎ 01439 798340

Osmotherley

OS Grid reference SE 456972

An ancient village that was a favourite location for smugglers trading in contraband from the coast. There is a stone cross and table in the centre. Grimshaw and Scotch Will visited on 19 July 1752 when they were paid one shilling and threepence (6p) expenses. They probably preached standing on the stone table in the centre of the village. This is also where

John Wesley first preached in Osmotherley at the invitation of a Roman Catholic priest. It is likely that Grimshaw and Scotch Will later preached in the Methodist chapel, John Wesley certainly did. This chapel (opened 1754) after a period of misuse has now been so modernised inside that it bears no resemblance to the former building. For access phone Mary Priest ☎ 01609 883497. There are two pubs and a café in the centre of this attractive village.

Top: Methodist Chapel, Osmotherley (1754)—the outside is unchanged

Above: The preaching table in Osmotherley, where Grimshaw and Scotch Will preached in July 1752

Osmotherley by road

A684 from Northallerton 11 mi (17 km) A19 from Thirsk 6 mi (9 km)

Mount Grace Priory

OS Grid reference SE 449985

England's most important Carthusian ruin. A reconstruction allows visitors to see the hermit-like isolation of the monks and their austere life style. Each cell has a study and bedroom on the ground floor opening into the monk's enclosed garden, and the second floor was his workshop. There is a herb garden, nature trail and picnic area.

Open November to March Wednesday to Sunday; April to October, daily. ☎ 01609 883494

Mount Grace by road

Just north of Osmotherley 12 mi (18 km) North of Thirsk, 7mi (10 km) North East of Northallerton on A19

Above: The Black Swan, Helmsley

Top: Mount Grace Priory

⑦ Roughed up at Roughlee

Grimshaw suffered emotional and physical blows but they failed to deter him from his calling. He won a war of words with George White after being attacked by his 'army'

Grimshaw travelled with Benjamin Ingham and his assistant William Batty to take a service in a house in Colne on 7 July 1747. They noticed a threatening crowd gathering round their leader and vicar, George White, at the entrance to a tavern and when the three entered the house they expected trouble— and it soon came. They had just begun to sing the opening hymn when White and the mob forced their way in and went for Batty. The three escaped into another room and overheard the vicar and constable threaten the householder with the stocks. As they attempted to carry him out, the man asked what authority they had to do this. The constable admitted that he had no warrant and promptly released him. The people who had gathered for the

Above: In July 1748 George White preached against the Methodists here in St Bartholomew's

Facing page: The Market Cross (replica), Colne

service fled in panic and White and the constable tried to persuade Grimshaw and Ingham to sign a promise not to preach in Colne again. When they refused to do so, they and Batty were dragged out of the house, pelted with mud and imprisoned in the *Swan Inn* (demolished c. 1937)

until White decided to release them.

On another occasion, William Batty was besieged at the meeting house in Clough. The mob broke down the doors and dragged him to White in Colne who again imprisoned him for the night. The following morning the mob frog-

Extracts from the battle of words

White's Sermon 24 July 1748:

'These Methodist preachers are authors of confusion, open destroyers of the public peace, flying in the face of the very church they may craftily pretend to follow, occasioning many bold insurrections, which threaten our spiritual government; schismatical rebels against the best of churches; authors of a further breach into our unhappy divisions; contemners of the great command, six days shalt thou labour etc. ... Poor ignorant men who never have been conversant further than the plough; who little know the constitution of any church, may be easily led astray by visionary notions about religion ... They really are unacquainted with the nature of preaching and instructing ... Industrious trade also, in

Above: St Bartholomew's where George White preached his sermon against the Methodists in July 1748

consequence of so many constant attendances on this model of worshipping the Creator will become an idle concern ... Consider how family affairs will suffer an inevitable neglect which may unfortunately prevent the education of children ...'

William Grimshaw's *Answer* in 1749—his only published work:

'The very tinkers and colliers of your parish have of late acted the parson as well as you

have done; and with as much regard to the truth and the honour of God ... Methodism, so called by way of reproach, is a complete system of gospel truths, and a perfect summary of reformation principles ... It has all the marks and indications of a divine work. It ascribes the total of man's salvation to the mere grace of God, the sole merits of Christ and the operation of the Holy Ghost.' (See page 105)

Above: *Farmhouse at Roughlee, one of the few remaining buildings from Grimshaw's time*

marched Batty to Justice Whitehead, who suggested to Batty that he should not preach again in Colne until he had obtained a licence: 'For you know they are a tumultuous and raging people.' White confirmed this by angrily shouting: 'I hope, Mr Whitehead, you do not encourage these men. I vow to God, before they preach in my parish, I'll sacrifice ye last drop of blood to root them out!'

White then preached and later published a sermon against the Methodists in which he sneered at them for being a weak and illiterate crowd, and warned that industry would suffer because of attendance at so many meetings.

It is difficult to assess the impact White's sermon had on its hearers. There would have been Methodists in the congregation, and others who would weigh his words against the dissolute life he led. Nevertheless, he seemed to be able to raise a rabble easily enough, given the proper inducements. Grimshaw went through White's sermon paragraph by paragraph refuting his argument in a magisterial way. There seems to be no doubt that William won the battle of words, but there is no proof that he changed anyone's opinion. There was a story that, dissipated by drink and on the point of death, White sent for Grimshaw and asked forgiveness.

Assaulted at Roughlee

John Wesley came to Haworth again in August 1748, on his way to preaching at Church Bank Bradford where: 'None behaved indecently except the curate of the parish'—although Wesley did arrive with a cut and bruised cheek from a stone thrown at Halifax. He preached on the

Wednesday evening to more than the church could contain and again at five in the morning to a church nearly full—the early start for weekday services was to allow people to get to work on time. So, on Thursday 25th August he set off on horseback with Grimshaw and William Mackford to rendezvous with Thomas Colbeck at Roughlee. Their intention was to encourage the members of the Darney society there. On the last part of the journey they received frequent warnings that an armed mob was on its way from Colne to Roughlee. Wesley was afraid for Grimshaw, having seen others broken through violence, but he soon found William was ready to suffer anything for Christ's sake.

White had issued another of his recruiting proclamations to break up the Methodist meeting: 'Notice is hereby given, that if any man be mindful, to enlist in His Majesty's Service under the command of the Rev. Mr George White, Commander in Chief and

Above: The Old Hall at Roughlee where Alice Nutter, one of the Pendle Witches, is said to have lived. She was hanged for witchcraft 19 August 1612

Facing page, top: Grimshaw country—the Yorkshire moors

Facing page, bottom: Roughlee 'boasts' its connection with witches

John Bannister, Lieutenant General of his Majesty's Forces for the defence of the Church of England, and the support of the manufactury in and about Colne, both of which are now in danger, let him repair to the drumhead at the Cross, where each man shall receive a pint of ale in advance and all other proper encouragements.' This legal-sounding proclamation had no authority, nor had White and Bannister the right to use the name of the King to authorise their spurious titles—least of all their impressive military ranks. Perhaps White had been drinking

too much of the ale! Nevertheless, a large crowd, including women, did assemble and it set off for Roughlee armed with sticks and stones.

After the warnings, Wesley and his companions rode faster, hoping to finish a short service and be on their way back to Haworth before the rabble arrived. At Roughlee, the Haworth party met up with Thomas Colbeck, William Batty, who now lived there, and John Bennet who had also brought the widow Grace Murray, Wesley's fiancée. They arrived at the field before White's army but as Wesley began his address the mob surrounded the field and waded into them. The service was broken up and the leader of the rioters, the deputy constable, insisted that Wesley went with them to Barrowford. Grimshaw, Colbeck and Batty followed while Grace Murray, on Grimshaw's advice, stayed behind and spent the following hours praying with

some of the believers in the preaching house.

Wesley was in the custody of 'a rough fellow', Richard Bocock deputy constable, who had no warrant, but he and his friends were marched to the drumbeat the two miles over the hill to Barrowford and frequently jostled by the triumphant crowd. They were taken into the *White Bear* where the constable, James Hargrave, asked him to promise not to go to Roughlee again. Wesley said he would sooner cut off his hand than make such a promise. For this brave response he was knocked to the ground by some of the constable's henchmen. After two or three hours Wesley promised not to preach at Roughlee on this occasion, after which Hargrave tried to quieten the mob.

Wesley left the inn by the front door accompanied by Hargrave, whilst Grimshaw and Colbeck slipped out at the back but were immediately violently attacked by the mob. Grimshaw broke free from his assailants but when he saw Colbeck being kicked by White's men he muscled his way through the crowd picked up Colbeck and shouted, 'Get out of the way Tommy with thy spindle-shanks [thin legs], let them kick me'—and took his place on the floor. Eventually they all got away,

though badly bruised and Grimshaw had had his wig stolen.

William Mackford and others were also badly beaten regardless of whether they were men or women. Mackford had been left for dead by the rioters, but fortunately survived. People were dragged by the hair, beaten with clubs and pursued as they tried to escape. One man jumped twelve feet down into the rocky river by the roadside to prevent being thrown in head first.

The death of Jane
Following the events at Roughlee, John Wesley took Grimshaw's children to Kingswood, the school he supervised in Bristol. The regime was very strict there but offered a better education than they could have expected in

Above: The early Methodists met here at Roughlee and later built a chapel that was demolished about 1970 because it was unsafe

Above: The White Bear (1607) where, in 1748, Grimshaw, Wesley and their companions were beaten-up by a mob encouraged by the local vicar, George White

Haworth. Fifteen months later, Grimshaw's daughter Jane died and William did not receive the news until she had been buried for a fortnight. The letter that his son John had written to his father said that she had trusted Jesus some time earlier. Grimshaw visited the grave at St Philip and St James' church in Bristol and took the unhappy son home with him. John, now a teenager, was showing behavioural problems and probably wanted more attention than his father had been able to give. Grimshaw apprenticed him to a godly man, John Greenwood, who had a weaving business at Bridgehouse on the river Worth at the foot of the hill on which Haworth was built. John, however, was lazy and indisciplined, perhaps because he knew that when he was twenty-one he would inherit his grandfather's property and would not need to work. His subsequent drunkenness and wild living would pain Grimshaw for the rest of his life.

Wesley demands justice

John Wesley was used to persecution but there must have been something about the one at Roughlee that really annoyed him. He wrote a letter to the constable in which he declared, 'Proceed against us if you can or dare; but not by lawless violence, not by making a drunken, cursing, swearing, riotous mob both judge and jury and executioner. This is flat rebellion against God and the King.' Wesley asked for an assurance that there would be no repeat of the trouble, but he cannot have had a satisfactory reply because he then instituted criminal proceedings against White for inciting riots. Although Grimshaw had counselled against

Above: Crossroads in Roughlee—now a village scattered laterally along the river bank

Below: The weir at Roughlee—perhaps the spot where a man jumped for his life

this, he did support Wesley in the case. However, whilst the jury at Preston Sessions found in favour of White, the bench favoured Wesley—the result being that White escaped punishment and the Methodists lost money.

Grimshaw's unpublished writings, written in exercise books, reveal the man more than his 'Answer' does. Like the 'Answer', they are now in the John Rylands University Library in Manchester. In *The Nature, State and Conduct of the Christian* he wrote: 'The true Christian is a humble man. He is a friendly enemy to himself: for though he be not out of favour with himself, no man esteems him less than himself, not out of ignorance or negligence but a voluntary meek dejectedness … His eyes are full of other men's perfections and his own wants. He would rather honour than be honoured.' This is so true of the services Grimshaw himself held at 'Sowdens', often

Right: The river from the bridge at Roughlee

on Saturday evenings. Visiting preachers hoping to hear him were usually pressed into preaching themselves. The compensation for them was Grimshaw's encouragement, which they would never forget.

Encouraging other preachers

William Thompson, who became the first president of the Methodist Conference following John Wesley's death in 1791, turned up at Haworth on his way to Scotland. He was an Irishman in his early twenties who had just been accepted by Wesley. As soon as he arrived, Grimshaw said, 'You must preach today, sir, in my little chapel.' Thompson protested that he had been hoping to hear Grimshaw, but like the others, he ended up preaching. Afterwards Grimshaw announced to all present: 'There is preaching for you! I will match him against the country! Yes, against the country!' When the lay preacher Benjamin Beanland visited, Grimshaw made him preach also. As he concluded, Grimshaw embraced him and said, 'The Lord bless thee, Ben! This is worth a hundred of my sermons!' Later, John Newton, a converted slave-trader, and now a custom official in Liverpool, came to Haworth. He believed he was called to preach but a few failures meant that he had lost confidence. Grimshaw insisted on him preaching, and the encouragement he received afterwards went a long way towards restoring the call and giving Newton the confidence for the great ministry he later exercised.

Colne

OS Grid reference SD 880400

Colne's history goes back to pre-Roman times. It developed in the Middle Ages through the wool trade, coal, and then a greater development through the cotton mills in Waterside to the South. It was also famous for producing black silk hats. Surprisingly for an inland town it has connections with two maritime disasters. Captain Barcroft enlisted men from Waterside, a district of Colne, to fight the French in the West Indies. In 1743, their ships were

Above: Bust of Wallace Hartley by the war memorial

Above: Bridgehouse, Haworth, where John Grimshaw was apprenticed

Above: *Pendle Heritage Centre is set in a picturesque range of Grade II listed buildings known as Park Hill which lie by the bridge in Barrowford.*

wrecked off Portland in a violent storm and all 226 men were lost. There is also a bust of Wallace Hartley in the town; he was leader of the band on the 'Titanic' and went down on the ship as they were playing 'Nearer My God to Thee'.

St Bartholomew's Church was founded 60 years after the Norman Conquest. The present building was intended to be built about 0.5 mi (1 km) from the present site but the legend tells that every day's stone laying was removed at night and expertly laid where the present church stands. Eventually finding they were not making any progress at the old site

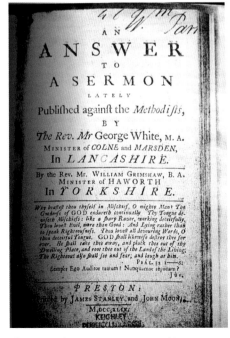

Above: Grimshaw's Answer to George White (see page 96)

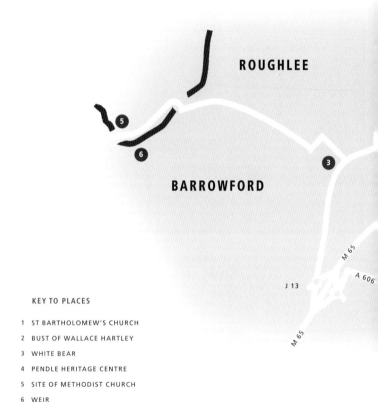

ROUGHLEE

BARROWFORD

M 65

A 606

J 13

M 65

KEY TO PLACES

1 ST BARTHOLOMEW'S CHURCH

2 BUST OF WALLACE HARTLEY

3 WHITE BEAR

4 PENDLE HERITAGE CENTRE

5 SITE OF METHODIST CHURCH

6 WEIR

the masons continued the building where it now stands. There were no gates or railings round the churchyard until 1820 and it was used for social occasions, but when someone died after hitting his head on a gravestone during a wrestling match it was decided to fence off the graveyard. Offenders, who in Grimshaw's days included Methodist preachers, used to be placed in the stocks here on market days. When the church bells were rung to commemorate the battle of Waterloo in 1815, one ringer was too enthusiastic; he raised his bell too high with the result that it swung over and fell, jerking him off his feet and up into the belfry. Fortunately, his head missed the beams but made a two-inch dent in the plaster ceiling.

Roughlee

OS grid reference SD 845403

Barrowford

OS Grid reference SD 850390

There is a visitor centre and tourist information shop here.

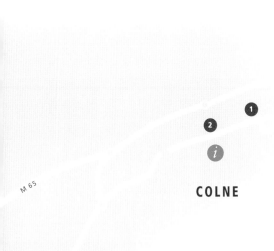

M 65

A 56

1

2

i

COLNE

Left: *Built in 1804 to collect tolls along the Marsden-Long Preston Turnpike Road, the old Toll House is now a delightful holiday cottage in Barrowford*

Above: Entrance to Pendle Heritage Centre

❽ An Unprofitable Servant

Increasing work, a worn out body, constant opposition and disputes within the ranks of his friends—the Methodists— each brought his life nearer to its close. The coup de grace came with the dreaded plague

G rimshaw's favourite text was 'For me to live is Christ, and to die is gain' (Philippians 1:21), it was inscribed on one of the flagons he gave to Haworth church, and on the Methodist chapel he had built in Haworth. The chapel was probably not used during Grimshaw's lifetime—why should it be with Grimshaw just down the street! However, he had it built in case his successor would not preach the Gospel.

Opposing revelry

Haworth had two 'feasts' or fairs each year. The last one included illegal horse racing on a rough plateau called Penistone Flats and was renowned for its drunkenness and licence. In 1759 Grimshaw told the organisers that they should abandon this practice but they refused. He then set up counter attractions but unfortunately, they did not attract the people who went to the feast, so he resorted to specific prayer that the races be stopped. There followed a frightening storm that lasted for three days! This so impressed the organisers that they never held another race there and it was popularly believed that it had been a direct divine

Above: There are still many rough tracks such as this around Haworth, used over the centuries by generations of inhabitants

Facing page: Entrance to the Brontë chapel in St Michael and All Angels, Haworth

Above: Part of West Lane Methodist Chapel Haworth

Below: The Dedication to Grimshaw on West Lane Methodist Chapel

intervention in response to 'old Grimshaw's prayers'.

Grimshaw started attending other fairs in the area, together with about six preachers, and they would preach the gospel throughout the fair. He took Bennet and some others to the Luddenden feast where they took it in turns to preach and sing hymns. The louder they sang, the louder the local band played and the more shotguns were discharged. Bennet recalled it sounded like a battle between the English and French armies.

John Grimshaw reached adulthood and inherited his granddad's estate. Ewood, which had been used as a staging post for preachers and for the occasional large meeting, now became John's residence and an open house for dissolute young people like himself. Although they had such success elsewhere, Grimshaw's pleadings for his son to flee from the wrath to come and to place his life into the hands of Jesus fell on deaf ears. John's behaviour openly defied his father's authority and added to the pressures William had to deal with.

Still prone to temptation
Besides all the external activity, Grimshaw was still suffering with his 'constitutional weakness' and succumbing to temptation, despite the guilt it brought: 'When

Above: A scene close to where the Penistone races were held. The exact location is now unknown—evidence of the effectiveness of Grimshaw's action in praying against them!

we give way to temptation there is always a consenting of the will, so an immediate gloominess and trouble covers the soul; this is that veiling of God's countenance which is greater or less as the consent is greater or less and a longer or less interval before we are received to pardon and favour … these are Fatherly chastisements.' We are indebted to the transparent honesty with which he wrote about his struggles revealing that even zealous Christians are not free of temptation and failure. It should be remembered that Grimshaw was a vigorous man who had chosen to be without the comforts a wife can offer in order to serve the Lord, and that choice inevitably placed strains on him: 'I have often found by simply touching a woman's hand, talking in a trifling way … or by touching their garments in a modest manner, lust arose, which by looking at too long has brought guilt, darkness, loss of God's presence, condemnation and grief upon my soul … I have been brought to walk heavily many a day; to vow and protest in the most solemn manner to Almighty God through his divine assistance to do so no more, but to be wholly given up in chastity, purity and holiness to him; and have as constantly broken that solemn engagement … I have often thought I shortly should, or really already had, so grieved the Lord in me that he would utterly and everlastingly forsake me.'

However, his experience was that the grace of God could use even these dark days for his glory: 'The more we are tempted, the faster we are rooted and stablished in the faith. At first, young

Right: Grimshaw's seventeenth century communion table in Brontë chapel

Facing page: Grimshaw's candelabra in the Brontë Chapel. The inscription reads: 'William Grimshaw A.B. To me to live is Christ, to die is gain 1759'

Christians are ready to faint under them … but in process of time, they learn their profitableness, and are not so desirous to be rid of them (for no cross, no crown) or that they may always have strength to bear, resist, or overcome them.'

Disagreement within Methodism

There were also problems among the Methodists; some were leaving and taking pastorates of Independent churches. Many lay preachers could not understand why they should be barred from conducting services of Holy Communion, and John Wesley was ready to ordain some of his preachers, presumably so they could administer the sacrament, but Charles together with Grimshaw opposed it. Grimshaw was against it because such a move would inevitably cause a break with the Church of England and, 'For my part, should this scheme take place, I must leave the Methodists; for I am determined to live and die in close communion as a member and minister of the Church of England.' The matter was adjourned to the next Conference.

At the Methodist Conference in 1755, Grimshaw's opinion was unchanged, much to the surprise

---

Excerpts from some of Grimshaw's re-dedications

June 1756: 'And conformable with my many former vows and dedications of myself to God … I do most solemnly and eternally give up, devote and dedicate myself spirit, soul and body to my dear and ever blessed triune God … And to this my solemn dedication and vow I do hereby solemnly invoke as witnesses thereto all the powers of heaven—God the Father, Son and Holy Ghost: all the holy angels and all the souls and spirits of just men made perfect: all the powers and solemn things on earth: the church, the Word of God, the Lord's Supper, men, earth, living creatures, sun moon and stars: and if it matter any thing, all that is in hell too, devils and all damned souls, to of those who were coming new to the debate, as they had always seen him as a peacemaker, trying to heal breaches with Whitefield and also with Ingham. Grimshaw was thought to be much more willing to compromise in order to retain peace and to be one of the most humble ministers, but here he was, opposing a breach with the Church of England in the strongest terms. The truth was that he was willing to compromise on opinions that did not affect the preaching of the gospel, but was not willing to concede on what he saw to be fundamental issues.

The plague strikes again

The strenuous lifestyle of this venturing preacher was beginning to take its toll. He had once written about the Christian: 'In short he lives and dies that Satan has no such match, sin no such enemy and God no such servant as he.' That well summed up his own commitment. However, by 1762 he was writing to Mrs Gallatin, his chief correspondent, that his health was impaired: 'And no wonder. I may say, as we do of a drunkard, "I live too fast to live long." I am a wonder to myself, that I am not in worse health than I am; or even that I am alive… I am seldom free from pain in my limbs and bowels. I write even now in pain.'

The plague, probably typhus—a disease of cold areas where people live in overcrowded and unsanitary conditions—is spread from one patient to another by body lice that live in clothing. It

bear witness to this renewal of this my solemn dedication and vow to God …'

Five weeks later: 'Having had again been thrice tempted in the like manner … I now renew it … resolved through the divine assistance, craved as above, to violate and renew it no more, so long as I live.'

A further 3 weeks later: '… again twice tempted … I once more and for ever (not intending to renew again, or give occasion for it) solemnly devote body soul and spirit.'

The covenants were renewed quarterly with fasting, the last one being in December 1762 after which he wrote: 'I believe that all true believers will be daily tempted by the flesh, as well as by the world and the devil, even to their lives' end.'

came to Haworth about every five years and struck the village again at the end of the winter of 1763. Grimshaw had a strong premonition that one of his household was going to die so he called them together and pleaded with them to ensure they were right with God. William continued to visit the sick as he was their pastor, anxious to take every opportunity to encourage their spiritual welfare.

On Sunday 20 March 1763 he preached his last sermon at Haworth. The following day the fever suddenly hit him and William recognised the illness from the last time he had it, when it had taken Elizabeth. It was unusual for anyone to have typhus twice as those who survive normally have lifetime immunity—perhaps William's restless lifestyle had increased his vulnerability. His high fever would alternate with chills, there would be general pain and severe exhaustion and after five or six days a black spot would appear on his upper torso and spread over the rest of his body apart from his face, palms and the soles of his feet. Recognising that his premonition was to do with his own death, William asked that he be given a poor man's burial suit and coffin. Regardless of the danger to themselves, there was a constant stream of visitors to his bedside. He still preached to the unconverted and exhorted the believers, not with his characteristic vehemence, but with a strong assurance from a heart at peace.

Many left his bedside encouraged and with Grimshaw's blessing on them. Jeremiah Robertshaw, a newly appointed preacher, heard him say, 'The Lord bless you, Jerry: I will pray for you as long as I live: and if there be such a thing as praying in heaven, I will pray for you there also.'

When Ingham made his second visit to the bedside, he brought a

INCUMBENTS
HAWORTH PARISH CHURCH

Name	Year
J. COLLIER, Royalist	1654
J. GARFORTH or Garton	1654
R. TOWN, Puritan	1645
J. COLLIER, Reinstated	1662
E. MORE	1677
R. MARGERISON, A. B.	1684
T. BLISONNE, A. M.	1702
W. CLIFFORD or CLIFFE, M. A.	1705
J. JACKSON, A. M.	?
J. SMITH, A. M.	1726
W. GRIMSHAW, A. B.	1742
J. RICHARDSON, M. A.	1763
J. CHARNOCK, M. A.	1791
S. REDHEAD, M. A.	1819
P. BRONTE, B. A.	1820
J. WADE, M. A.	1861
T. W. STORY, M. A.	1898
G. A. ELSON, M. A.	1919
J. C. HIRST, M. A.	1925
W. T. DIXON, B. A. (CANON)	1947
E. A. BARTON	1959
C. MANCHESTER, B. D.	1961
R. T. HUGHES, B. A.	1967
R. F. ASHDOWN, M. A.	1974
C. SPIVEY	1985
P. J. SLATER, M. A.	1993
J. A. SAVAGE, DIP.TH, RS	2002

Above: *Wooden board displaying the names of ministers at Haworth parish church, including Grimshaw.*
J. Collier, a Royalist, was expelled during Cromwell's Commonwealth; Robert Town, a Puritan, was ejected on 24 August 1662 for refusing to comply with the 1662 Act of Uniformity

Above: Scotch Will's cottage remained uninhabited after his death in 1779. Recently it was renovated and is now a private building accessed by a private road

message from the Countess of Huntingdon. Grimshaw responded, 'Tell her Ladyship, that dear elect woman, that I thank her from the bottom of my heart for all her kindnesses to me over the years I have known her. With my dying breath I implore every blessing temporal and spiritual to rest upon her. May the God of Abraham, of Isaac, and of Jacob, bless her—bless her in body, soul and spirit. I can never repay the spiritual good I have reaped at her hands. O that she may be eminently useful in her day and generation!' He was silent for a long time and then said, 'I am quite exhausted, but I shall soon be at home, for ever with the Lord—a poor miserable sinner redeemed by his blood.'

The pain was more than he had ever experienced. Thomas Colbeck said that his body was so inflamed that it burnt as if he had been in an oven. Nevertheless, he told Henry Venn that he was as happy as he could be on earth and as sure of glory as if he was in it. He kept slipping into a coma, and after one said that he had had a more wonderful visit from God than he had ever known. So this was an experience greater than that in the *Black Bull*, but he was either too weak, or words were not sufficient to describe it.

'Here goes an unprofitable servant'

William died on 7 April 1763 aged 55, almost three weeks after falling ill. In the morning he had told Molly his maid that the previous night he had suffered like the martyrs, his flesh had been as if it was roasting before a fire: 'But I have nothing to do but to step out of my bed into heaven. I have my foot on the threshold already.' His last words were, 'Here goes an unprofitable servant!' He had been twenty-one years at Haworth.

Grimshaw's friends were afraid he would die penniless because he was so generous. He used to ask for cast off boots, pay for them to be repaired, and give them to the poor. He would take food from his own table for the hungry, and sometimes had no change of clothing when he returned home drenched from a visit. However, he was able to leave Molly, his housekeeper, five pounds and although William left little for his son to inherit, he did get his old grey mare. John used to say to it: 'Once you carried a saint, but now you carry a devil.' This and the scene of serenity at his father's bedside were working a change in him and he gradually began to seek after God. John was only thirty years old when he fell seriously ill. A man who came to pray for him said that he had found peace with God. Just before he died John said, 'What will my father say when he sees me in heaven!'

The funeral

On the 8 April 1763 Grimshaw's body was slung between two horses in single file leading a procession of many of his congregation over the moors to Ewood, now the home of his son John and his wife. The coffin was inscribed with William's favourite text: 'For me to live is Christ, and to die is gain'. There was a good deal of weeping but also confident hymn singing on the journey. The following day, April 9th, the cortege processed down the hill to the church at Luddenden, singing the Psalms that he had chosen: 23, 39 and 91. The church was packed and he was laid to rest next to Sarah beneath the chancel. The people

Other preachers go to their reward

William Darney continued to be persecuted and to be in trouble with the Methodist hierarchy wherever he went. He died in his little house by Pendle Hill in 1779.

Thomas Mitchell was stationed in Staffordshire and Kent and then Keighley where he died in 1785 aged 59: 'I look back on the labour of three and thirty years … and am not grown weary either of my Master, or the work I am engaged in. Though I am weak in body, and in the decline of life, my heart is still engaged in the cause of God. I am never more happy than when I feel the love of Christ in my heart and am declaring his praise to others.'

Above: Churchyard at Luddenden

Facing page: Grimshaw and Sarah together again

then returned to Ewood for a dinner and then back to the church for the sermon on his favourite text. The preacher was Henry Venn who in 1759 had come to be vicar of Huddersfield, just over twenty miles from Haworth. Although he had known for only a few years the man he called: 'That burning and most shining light, dear Mr Grimshaw' they often met during that time and he was one of the visitors during William's last illness. The church was so full that Venn had to address the mourners in the graveyard. The following day, Sunday, he repeated the sermon from Grimshaw's pulpit at Haworth.

John Nelson died in 1774. 'His remains were carried through the streets of Leeds … attended by thousands who were either singing or weeping. It was truly a very solemn season to many, to see him carried to his grave, who had done so much and suffered so much in these parts for the honour of God and the good of men.'

After 50 years as a Christian he said, 'I am more in love with his service than ever.'

Outliving most of his fellow preachers, Jonathan Maskew died aged 81. He often urged Christians to keep up their 'private trade with heaven,' and added, 'A Christian can as well live without food, see without eyes, or walk without feet, as to live to God without secret prayer.'

Venn said that it was hard on that occasion to determine, 'Whether we have more cause to lament his removal from the world; or to rejoice that God was pleased to enrich him with divine knowledge in so large a measure, to make him so long an eminent instrument in his hand of converting sinners, and to enable him to persevere with such unblemished character, till he finished his course with joy.'

Henry Venn claimed that many Christians know what it is to be born again: 'But few of that happy number have expressed so great ardency of affection to the service of Christ as your late much-loved pastor … He never asked, like a double-minded man, what the careless, the profane, or self-righteous would say of him or what they might do to him. The truth of God he stood valiantly in defence of, defying mockery or threats, opposition and hatred. Ye are all his witnesses, that an unreserved obedience to Christ was the very joy of his heart.'

Speaking of the joy of the Lord, Venn continued: 'More of this joy very few possessed than dwelt in your deceased pastor, so justly beloved by you all. His very countenance proclaimed that the joy of the Lord was his strength. Who among you ever joined with him in any part of worship, without a proof that his heart was engaged in it with great delight? … What were his sermons but animating persuasives from one who took pleasure in speaking

Above: Main Street, Haworth

Above: A quiet corner behind the church at Haworth

good of his Master's name … Which of you ever received with him the Holy Communion without perceiving it was an exquisite feast of joy to his soul?'

Grimshaw, because of his outstanding personality and gifts had been hero-worshipped by many. Dan Taylor, an ex-Methodist, who founded the New Connexion of General Baptists, expressed the thought that God might have removed him because people had tended to 'forget the Lord and idolise the saint.'

Hundreds came to Christ through William's ministry. Some became Baptists and others Independents and although his desire was for revival of the Church of England, he was happy to have fellowship with all who sincerely loved Christ. His influence on Venn and others continued through godly ministers in the Church of England such as Charles Simeon and Venn's own son John, vicar of Clapham, who had William Wilberforce and other prominent social reformers and missionary workers in his congregation.

When John Newton stood with Grimshaw on Penistone hill overlooking Haworth in 1760, it was their last meeting. What William told him there summarises the extent of his evangelism and the depth of his pastor's heart for his people. He said that when he had first arrived he could have gone half a day's journey to any point of the compass without meeting a true Christian, but now by the grace of God there were several hundreds there. He knew the temptations and trials of nearly all his communicants as well as if he had lived in their families.

TRAVEL INFORMATION

Ewood

OS Grid reference SE 021262

This is where Ewood Hall and Court the home of the Lockwoods used to be. There is a private building, divided into apartments, that is called Ewood Court but this is Victorian and said to be built where the old Court stood. It has a summer house that predates the building and John Wesley is said to have preached there but this is now private property.

Ewood in Midgley by road

Take the A646 from Todmorden and take the road signed 'Midgley' off left in Mytholmroyd.

Luddenden

OS Grid reference SE 042261

So deep between the Pennines in the Calderdale valley that it gets little sun after October.

By Road

Take the A646 from Todmorden and turn left in Luddenden Foot at the traffic lights.

Above and opposite:
The North Yorkshire Moors is the largest expanse of heather moorland in England and Wales. Within its 55,000 hectares there are over seven hundred ancient monuments and three thousand listed buildings

Below: A mile marker on the Rochdale Canal which was reopened in 1996

BIBLIOGRAPHY

Cook, F., *William Grimshaw of Haworth*, Banner of Truth, Edinburgh 1997 ISBN 0 85151 7323

Longworth, A., *William Grimshaw* Methodist Publishing, Peterborough (booklet) 1996 ISBN 1 85852 055 X

Skevington-Wood, A., *William Grimshaw of Haworth*, Evangelical Library (pamphlet) 1963

Acknowledgements

Christine Bradley, Christine Carradine, Jane Helliwell, John and Anne Lowcock, Dr Peter Nockles and staff at John Rylands University Library, Manchester, Pam Riding, Steve Taylor and Doreen Wyllie for their help with aspects of the research.

The Author

 Fred Perry has written two books based on research while Cropwood Fellow at the University of Cambridge Institute for Criminology. He was minister at Frizinghall Congregational Church, had a shared ministry and was later Moderator of Lister Hill Baptist Church, Leeds, where he is still a member. Retiring on health grounds after fifteen years as an adviser with the Central Council for Education and Training in Social Work, he became Hon. Secretary and trustee of the Leeds European Refugee Trust which was instrumental in bringing 500 refugees to Britain during the Bosnian war. Married for fifty years, he and Jean have four children, fourteen grandchildren, eight great grandchildren—and counting!

A SUMMARY OF GRIMSHAW'S LIFE

3 or 14 September 1708*	William Grimshaw born Brindle, Lancashire
1 May 1714	Begins schooling
November 1715	Jacobites defeated at nearby Preston
2 April 1726	Admitted to Christ's College Cambridge as a sizar
May 1727	Awarded scholarship at Christ's
3 November 1730	Awarded Bachelor of Arts
4 April 1731	Ordained deacon, impressed by the service
April—September 1731	Curate at Littleborough
17 September 1731	Begins ministry at Todmorden
10 September 1732	Ordained priest, Chester Cathedral
9 June 1735	Marries Sarah Sutcliffe
April 1736	Son John born
March 1737	Daughter Jane born
1 November 1739	Wife Sarah dies
26 November 1739	Writes 'form of my burial'
13 August 1741	Marries Elizabeth
16 May 1742	Becomes perpetual curate of Haworth
June 1742	Twelve communicants at Haworth
1743	Grimshaw begins monthly visitations within his parish
January 1744	Grimshaw meets Scotch Will
2 September 1744	Vision in the Black Bull

November 1745	Jacobite rebels in Pendle forest
December 1745	Jacobite army retreats to Scotland
22 October 1746	Charles Wesley visits, William and Elizabeth ill
October/November 1746	Elizabeth dies
1747	William begins his 'circuit' work
May 1747	John Wesley visits Haworth
7 July 1747	William, Ingham and Batty mobbed at Colne
25 May 1748	Grimshaw faces charges at Wakefield
24 July 1748	White preaches against the Methodists
25 August 1748	Grimshaw, John Wesley and others at Roughlee
August 1748	William's children taken to Kingswood school
1747	Grimshaw's answer to White's sermon
14 January 1750	William's daughter Jane dies
January 1750	Grimshaw takes son John home
September 1752	Scotch Will excluded from conference in Leeds
September 1762	Grimshaw writes that he is in pain
7 April 1763	William dies
9 April 1763	Buried with Sarah at Luddenden
10 April	Venn repeats funeral sermon at Haworth

* All Roman Catholic countries changed their calendar from the Julian to the more accurate Gregorian scheme in the 17th century. England and America did not make the adjustment until 1752, which meant that in that year Wednesday 2 September was followed by Thursday 14 September. So, the exact anniversary of William's birth fell on 3 September until 1752 when it became 14 September.

TRAVEL NOTES

The following notes are for those who are new to visiting places of interest, and especially for overseas visitors; a little information about your host country will make you feel more at home and less of a stranger.

1 What do you wear?

Travelling on public transport can be hot and dirty; so it is better to dress comfortably rather than smartly – especially footwear. Wear thin layers topped with a light waterproof that can protect from wind as well as rain. It is easier to carry two or more thinner garments than a heavy coat and jumper. Remember that the only reliable thing about the British weather is that it is unreliable.

2 Take great care with personal belongings.

Keep wallets and purses out of sight on your person – bags can easily be snatched. Cameras and other personal items should be kept secure at all times. A rucksack may be good for your back, but in crowds it can be opened and items removed without your

knowledge. Never put a bag down and walk off, it is a security hazard and will probably have disappeared when you return. Don't assume that your property is more secure because you are in the heart of rural Britain.

*For overseas visitors.

Do not carry your passport with you, unless you plan to change money. Hotels have a safe where you can store valuables. Carry a photocopy of the relevant pages of your passport; if the original is lost then it will be easier for your embassy to issue a temporary document.

3 Obtain a map of public transport in

the area you are travelling. Basic maps are free from tourist information kiosks; bus and railway maps are available from bus and railway stations.

4 Always respect the places you visit.

Take note of 'No Entry' and 'Private' signs. A private dwelling may once have had a connection with the subject of this book, but please do not disturb the present residents. Usually there will be an indication at the property if it is open for public viewing.

5 Photography.

Respect any 'Photography not permitted' signs. In some museums and historic buildings you may take photographs, but you are not permitted to use a tripod since this can be very annoying to other visitors. Bear this in mind when deciding on the speed of film you buy. You may be able to use a monopod, but always enquire first to save hassle. You are well advised not to buy film from a street vendor, however cheap it may appear; old or poor quality film can

... ruin your valuable memories. Always buy film or Flash cards in a reputable shop, and always keep the receipt.

6 In a museum, exhibition or church

do not touch anything that you are not permitted to handle. Not only can an object be damaged, but also in certain circumstances prosecution may result.

7 Respect graves in a cemetery, church or

churchyard. Please be careful not to cause offence, especially if a service is taking place or if someone is sitting quietly by a grave.

8 When walking in the countryside

please respect the country code. Leave gates as you

found them – whether open or closed. Keep to the paths, or walk around the edge of fields. Do not drop litter – farm animals are not smart and will chew on your discarded litter, often with tragic results. If you have a dog with you, ensure that it does not worry any livestock. Never light a fire.

9 Litter.
Please be careful with the disposal of all litter

including gum. Reference libraries and museums may ask you to remove gum if they see you chewing.

10 You will probably find it useful to put together a tourist pack. We

suggest the following: a notebook, a pen or pencil, a small torch with batteries that work and a small medical kit.

11 Eating out. For most trips you may

prefer to take a packed lunch. City eating places can be expensive. If a hot meal is required there are many different types of food outlets to suit all tastes and styles. Many Garden Centres have excellent cafeterias or restaurants and are usually good value for money. These are normally open for food

The British Museum, London

between 1000 and 1600 hours. Good rural public houses can also provide quality service.

12 Disabled visitors.

All public buildings in the UK are under a legal requirement to be wheelchair accessible; those

in charge of such places are usually very helpful, but in old buildings full access is not always possible.

13 Public conveniences

(restrooms). In cities these are usually open until about 1800 hours. Most major stores, large petrol (gas) stations, restaurants or cafés will have conveniences. Always carry tissues with you, as some public conveniences will not provide toilet tissue.

14 Especially for London

Because of the Congestion Charge and the difficulty of parking, we strongly advise you against taking a car into the centre of London.

The Congestion Charge

The congestion charge is £5 daily in 2004. The aim is to reduce traffic, making journeys and delivery times more reliable, and raise millions each week to re-

invest in London's transport system.

Who has to pay the charge?

There are some exemptions and discounts, but if you are due to pay and do not, a Penalty Charge Notice will be issued.

This website tells you about central London congestion charging and what you need to do.

Website: www.cclondon.com

Transport maps

A London combined network map—bus, underground (tube) and overland railway—is available from bus garages and railway stations; also many newsagents who display the London transport sign.

Travel to all London sites will be referred to from one of the main London termini. The best time to travel into London on a weekday is after 0930 hours. You can save money if your train leaves after this time, and you avoid the rush hour. The transport companies have divided London into zones, and the number of zones visited will determine the cost of the ticket. The best ticket to buy is a Travel Card (you can get daily, weekly or monthly cards) which will enable you to go by train, tube and bus all on the same ticket. Make sure that you buy the right ticket for the places to be visited; just ask the clerk in the ticket office.

If you are thinking of using **Buses in central London,** remember to buy your ticket before you travel. If you do not have a Travel Card which includes your bus fare, it will be necessary to buy a ticket from one of the **ticket machines which are at all central London bus stops.**

The ticket machines are very simple to use and sell Adult and Child single tickets as well as One Day Bus Passes

You'll need the exact money (as they don't give change) They take £2, £1, 50p, 20p, 10p and 5p coins.

A guide to using buses if you have a disability

An increasing number of low floor accessible buses are being introduced to London and currently run on more than 35 routes across the capital. They have a low flat floor to make travel easier for the elderly and disabled customers as well as those with pushchairs. For further information on routes, prices and frequency of tubes and buses in London, call 020 7222 1234

Refreshments in London

are many and various. It would be best to have a packed lunch as we suggest above, but if you prefer hot food, please take note of the following: Always check that the food and drink prices are listed before you place an order. Always query any discrepancies before payment is made. Drinks and food from road-side vendors in the cities will be more expensive.

Unless you have a good budget, the best places for light refreshments are fast food restaurants, especially if you just want a hot drink. Another possibility worth investigating is any café that builders are using! They may not be the most luxurious, but the workers normally know where to find good wholesome food, that it is served quickly and hot – and at a reasonable price.

Useful Telephone Numbers

In an emergency call **999** (you can also use **112**) and ask for Fire, Police or Ambulance. Tell the emergency service where the trouble is, what the trouble is, where you are and the number of the phone you are using. Please remember this is an **emergency service** and not an information service. Never make an unnecessary call.

If you need help in making a call that is Local or National, call free on **100**. If help is required in making an International call, call free on **155**.

If you require help in finding a number or code call Directory Enquiries, you will be charged for this service. For Local and National numbers there are a number of directory assistance numbers available, all of which charge for their service. You can call **118 118**, or **118 500.** Note that once directory assistance has located the number for you, they can connect you directly—but be aware that you will pay for the call at a higher rate!

For International directory enquiries call **153**.
Travelodge central reservations. 08700 850 950. www.travelodge.co.uk
Travel Inn central reservations. 0870 242 8000.
Tourist Information Centres www.mistral.co.uk/hammerwood/uk.htm
National rail enquiries: 08457 484950. Or for the hard of hearing, 08456 050600. www.rail.co.uk
London Transport 020 7 222 1234 www.londontransport.co.uk

DAY ONE TRAVEL GUIDES

For serious research as well as group outings

This series is unique: each book combines biography with travel guide. Notes, maps and photographs help you to explore Britain's distinctive heritage. The subjects covered in this series include John Bunyan, Charles Haddon Spurgeon, William Booth, John Knox, and Martyn Lloyd-Jones

For personal study at home

For individuals on the trail

128 PAGES   **£9.99 EACH**

★ PLACES OF INTEREST TO VISIT

★ PACKED WITH COLOUR PHOTOS

★ CLEAR ILLUSTRATED MAPS

★ GREAT GIFT IDEA

★ CALL DAY ONE: ☎ 01568 613 740